American Indians In Colorado:
Dancing With Grace

By
Dr. Karen D. Herndon

Karen D. Herndon Ed.D has been a classroom teacher, University professor specializing in social studies and multicultural aspects of education, Director of a Teacher Education program at the University of Colorado Denver, Director of Staff Development in a large metropolitan school district, and Dean of Academic Affairs at University College, University of Denver. Early in her career, a visit to Rough Rock School in the Navajo Nation led to her deep commitment to teaching about American Indians with historical and cultural accuracy. Working closely with Indian people, she has been a consultant to the Department of Indian Education in Denver Public Schools, writing curriculum including units on the Powwow, Thanksgiving, From the Beginning (American Indian history) and course syllabi. She has also been a consultant to the Denver Indian Center on educational issues. Some of her books for educators include *Indian Country, How To Teach About American Indians*, and *American Indian voices*. She has also reviewed approximately 75 new books about American Indians for ARBA/Libraries Unlimited, INC.

Self-Published by Dr. Herndon through
createspace.com and amazon.com

ISBN-13: 978-1477410943

ISBN-10: 1477410945

This book is written for my grandchildren Emma Eikermann, Kara Eikermann, Brian Harvey, and Valerie Harvey.

It is also written for the Indian children of Colorado.

It is written for Colorado teachers and parents too.

It is written in hope that all will continue to seek the rest of the story.

Table of Contents

Acknowledgements

This book could not have been written without the painstaking research of many scholars. Their scholarship provided the foundation of this book for children. As always, I am deeply grateful to Dr. Gary Knight, professor at Ft. Lewis College, and his family who first introduced me to the Navajo people of Rough Rock, Arizona. I am especially grateful for the continuing support of my friends RoseMarie McGuire, Director of Indian Education for Denver Public Schools and a strong, dedicated Dakota woman, and John Compton, a wise, generous, and humorous Lakota elder.

Two excellent teachers, Jennifer Morton and Sue Bryers, helped to ensure that the book was useful to teachers and engaging to children. Katrina Her Many Horses and her family, Ceriss Blackwood and her grandmother, and Dr. Sara Jumping Eagle graciously allowed me to tell their stories. Gracie Tyon, a teacher and Lakota Jingle Dress dancer and Powwow dance judge reviewed the powwow material. Don Williams, a friend, a photographer, and an Apple genius, taught me new skills, patiently fixed my mistakes and made this book a reality.

Four Big Ideas

- ■ The environment shapes cultures.
- ■ All cultures change over time.
- ■ When people from different cultures meet, they learn from each other.
- ■ When cultures have different beliefs, values, and goals, there is often conflict.

American Indians In Colorado:
Dancing With Grace

Chapter 1
Backwards from Now

As soon as she steps through the door of the Denver **Coliseum**, Grace feels at home. All around her are the people, the sounds, the smells, the colors, and the **traditions** that make her the person that she is. Everything here makes her feel safe and comfortable. The deep sounds of the drums and the songs of many nations fill her ears. Her feet want to dance. The smell of fry bread reminds her of good times with her family and friends. The rainbow of colors and styles of powwow regalia twirl and swirl around her like a kaleidoscope. She feels strong and proud. Grace will soon join the dancers and the American Indian people who came to the Denver March **Pow*Wow** from all over America. They came to celebrate their Indian cultures with singing, dancing, good food, and beautiful art.

Every year in March the Denver Coliseum is host to the Denver March Pow*Wow. This huge coliseum in Denver is filled with hundreds of American Indian dancers, drummers, war veterans, artists, people selling their goods, storytellers, American Indians, and **spectators**. This is a very large powwow. Indian people come from many states to participate. They come to meet their friends, to drum, to dance, to sing, and to celebrate their traditions.

The Powwow

Some powwows are large and people come from all parts of the nation to celebrate their Indian cultures. Many other powwows are small and are held in places like schools or churches. In the summer, many powwows are held outdoors. Some powwows have dance contests and prizes. Others are more spiritual or religious and people dance to celebrate or honor someone or to pray for themselves or other people.

Grace is ten years old and is in the fifth grade in Denver Public Schools. She is a member of the Southern Cheyenne Nation. Her culture is Southern Cheyenne and she is very proud of her people and their traditions. The powwow has many dance contests for men, women, boys, girls, and even very small children who are called tiny tots. The winners of the contests win prizes of money. Many Native cultures dance at the Powwow.

Grace is a Jingle Dress dancer and she will dance in

The Jingle Dress Dance

Every tribe has their own stories about the different dance styles. This is the most well-known legend of the Jingle Dress Dance.

A Medicine Man couldn't cure his people of the diseases that came west with the explorers and settlers. When he prayed, he was given a vision. He saw his daughter and her three friends dancing in dresses covered with "jingles." They danced around the sick person. In the dream, he was taught the healing songs. When he woke up, he showed his wife and daughter how to make the dresses. His people were cured when they danced the Jingle Dress Dance.

Long ago, the cones were carved out of wood. The jingles are now made of chewing tobacco lids. The jingle dress dance is one of the intertribal dance styles at powwows today. It is done for healing of the mind, heart, body, and soul.

*Adapted from: 26th Annual Denver March Pow*Wow: Program Guide. 2000.*

Regalia

American Indian dance clothing is called regalia, not costumes. Costumes are clothes
made to make someone look
different than who they are, like
wearing a clown or a pirate
costume.

*United Tribes Technical Col-
lege. 1993. Powwow: Questions
and answers. Bismarck, ND:
Author, p. 1.*

the Grand Entry and the Jingle Dress Dance contest. Her grandmother and her Aunt Rose spent many days sewing her **regalia**. She has been practicing at home and dancing at powwows at the Denver Indian Center and other small powwows held outside in the summer and fall.

The Grand Entry is a parade of all of the dancers who will compete in the contests. A powwow always begins with the Grand Entry. Because there are so many dancers, it takes a long time for them to form a line and enter the **arena**. As they enter, they dance in a circle winding around and around. Each drum group will sing for the dancers. When all the dancers are in the arena, it is filled with color, movement, sound, and pride.

As Grace waits for the Jingle dancers to enter the arena, she begins to think of the dancers all around her. How many people are from Colorado? Have their dances changed from long ago? How have Indian people changed from long ago? Why did they dance? How did they live before they had grocery stores, shopping malls, schools, and cars? How did their lives change after the explorers, traders, miners, and settlers came? How is her life in a city different from the lives of the people who live on Indian reservations? So many questions start to buzz around in her head!

Grace knows her grandparents and other elders can answer many of her questions. They tell wonderful stories from long ago. But her grandparents' stories are Southern Cheyenne stories and tell about her ancestors and her history. Where are the stories and history of the Ute people who were the first Indians to live in Colorado? What about stories and history of the Arapaho people? She knows that much of her Southern Cheyenne history is linked to Arapaho history but she doesn't know why.

Grace's questions are important and interesting too. These questions and their answers tell us about the history of Colorado. This book is going to take you backwards from now and then forward to the future. You will explore the past of American Indians in Colorado and discover how they lived then and now. You will learn how and why the lives of Indian people changed and how many of their beliefs and values stayed the same. And, you will find out if Grace wins a prize when she dances in the Jingle Dress Dance contest.

More Books to Read

Rendon, Marcie. R. *Powwow Summer: A Family Celebrates the Circle of Life.* Minneapolis, MN: Lerner, 1996.

Smith, Cynthia L. *Jingle Dancer.* New York, NY: Morrow, 2002.

Videos to Watch

Into the Circle: An Introduction to the Powwow. Tulsa, OK: Gull Circle Videos, 1992.

Places to Go

Denver March Pow*Wow

Any powwow in your city or town

Music to Hear

Kids' Pow-wow Songs Phoenix, AZ: Canyon Records,. 1996.

More Kids' Pow-Wow Songs. Phoenix, AZ: Canyon Records, 2005.

Websites to Visit

http://www.denvermarchpowwow.org

Definitions

Arena	a flat, round enclosed area where the Pow*Wow dancers dance
Celebration	the ceremonies or festivities held to observe a day or honor an event, a person, or a culture
Coliseum	a large building built for public events
Pow*Wow	an event where Indian people come together to be with friends, dance, feast, and trade. Some powwows are large and people come from all parts of the nation to celebrate their Indian cultures. Many other powwows are small and are held in places like schools or churches. In the summer, many powwows are held outdoors. Some powwows have dance contests and prizes. Others are more spiritual or religious and people dance to celebrate or honor someone or to pray for themselves or other people.
Regalia	the special clothing worn for powwow dancing
Spectators	people who watch an event

Traditions   ways of thinking, acting, celebrating, and believing that
                      are handed down from one generation to another

Types of Powwow Dances

- ■ Men's Traditional Dance
- ■ Men's Grass Dance
- ■ Men's Fancy Dance
- ■ Women's Traditional Dance
- ■ Women's Fancy Shawl Dance
- ■ Jingle Dress Dance
- ■ Intertribal Dances
- ■ Tiny Tots

The Powwow Circle

*The circle is an important symbol
to Native American people.*

*The dancers are in the center of a circle,
the drums and audience form a circle around them,
and the concessions form yet another circle around the gathering.*

*The Powwow brings the circle of the people closer together—
closer to their family, friends,
and their Native American culture.*

Roberts, Chris. People of the Circle *Missoula, MT: Meadowlark Publishing,
1998.*

Chapter 2
Colorado—Mother Earth

As Grace waits to dance with the Jingle Dress dancers in the Grand Entry, she wonders how American Indians in Colorado lived long ago. Today, her family lives in a small and comfortable house in Denver. Usually, her Mom shops for their groceries at the supermarket. Her family enjoys cooking dinner together one night a week. Spaghetti is their favorite! Almost every day, Grace and her brother David eat a hot lunch at school. On Saturday, they like to go to McDonald's for lunch. There are lots of ways their family gets the food they need.

When they need other things for their home and family, they go shopping at the big stores close to their house or they drive to the mall. If they go to the mall, they sometimes go to the movies too. Grace's dad always buys a big box of popcorn for everyone to share!

In the past, American Indian people couldn't go to McDonald's for hamburgers and milk shakes. They didn't have stores to buy other things they needed. There were no restaurants, grocery stores, hardware stores, drugstores, or shopping malls to buy food, furniture, blankets, clothes, toys, tools, and medicines. If people needed a new home for their families, they couldn't just rent or buy a house or apartment. They had to build a shelter or home. Where did they get food and clothing for their families? What kind of materials and tools did they need to build a home?

The answers to these questions were the same for Indian people, wherever they lived. They also were the same for people who were not Indian, wherever they lived. Long ago, all people used the land and the **natural resources** around them for their food, clothing, and shelter. The earth gave them the the things that they needed. It was their grocery store, their hardware store, their drugstore, their toy store, and their resource for all that they needed to **survive**.

Culture Areas

The **environment** (land and natural resources) are very important to how people lived their lives. When scientists study the lifeways of American Indian people who lived long ago, they divide North America into areas that have much the same environment called **Culture Areas**. Each environment or Culture Area has four important parts:

- ◼ **Landforms**–the shape of the land like **mountains, plateaus, plains**, lakes, and rivers
- ◼ **Elevation**–how far the land is above or below sea level
- ◼ **Climate**–the temperature, **precipitation** (rain and snow), and wind
- ◼ **Natural Resources**
  - ⊙ things on the land and in the air like trees, plants, animals, fish, birds, and insects
  - ⊙ things underground like gold, silver, coal, and other minerals

The landforms, elevation, climate, and natural resources are different in each Culture Area. In Colorado there are three Culture Areas. These three Culture Areas are only partly in Colorado. The **Great Plains Culture Area** covers most of the land on the Eastern side of the Rocky Mountains and along the Northern part of the state. The **Great Basin Culture Area** covers the Rocky Mountains and most of the Western side of the mountains. A very small area in the southern part of the state is in the **Southwest Culture Area**.

Each of these Culture Areas has a different kind of environment. Each environment shaped the lives of the people who lived there long ago. Why did the environment in each culture area make a difference in the lives of Indian people?

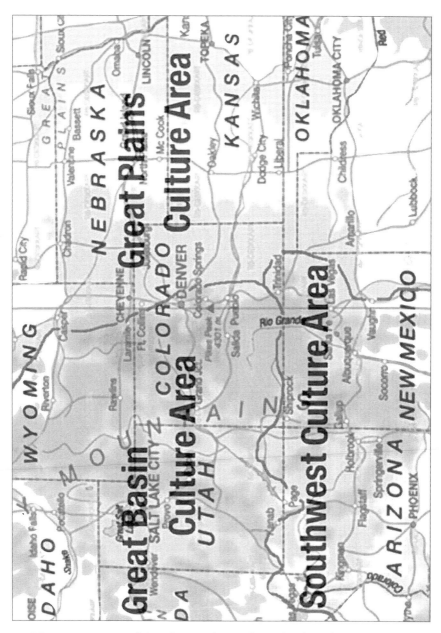

Here are some of the things the Indians had to think about long ago so they could survive in Colorado.

Food

- ▣ Where can we find food for our families?
- ▣ Where can we find plenty of animals and birds to hunt?
- ▣ Is there water for fishing and drinking?
- ▣ Where can I find nuts, seeds, roots, and berries to gather?
- ▣ Is the earth good for planting?
- ▣ Will plants have enough sun and rain to grow?
- ▣ Is it warm long enough for plants to grow strong?
- ▣ Is there enough good water for drinking and for growing plants?

Clothing

- ▣ What clothes do we need for protection?
- ▣ Do we need warm clothes for snow and cold weather?
- ▣ Are there enough animals for hides to make shoes and clothes?
- ▣ Are there plants that we can use for shoes or clothes?
- ▣ What can we use to decorate our clothes?

Shelter

- ▣ What kind of home do we need for our families?
- ▣ How can we make shade from the sun on hot days?
- ▣ Will our homes protect us from wind and snow?
- ▣ Do we need homes that we can move from place to place ?
- ▣ Can we live in one **permanent** place?
- ▣ Are there enough animal hides to make homes?
- ▣ Are there plenty of trees and wood to build homes?
- ▣ Are water and wood available close to our homes?

Trade

- ▣ How can we travel to other places to trade?

Indian people learned how to survive in each Culture Area in Colorado. They all had to have food, clothing, and shelter. So, they used the resources in each environment to meet these needs. Because the environment in each culture area was different, the traditions and lifeways of Indian people in Colorado developed in ways that were both alike and different.

The Indians in Colorado moved back and forth as they looked for food and the things that they needed. They would often trade with people who lived in other environments for things that were not available in their own environment. They would also borrow ideas from each other if a new idea seemed to work better than what they were doing.

The Great Plains Culture Area

The Great Plains Culture Area is very large. It stretches from Canada almost to Mexico. The Eastern part of Colorado is part of this Culture Area. This means that Indian people on the Plains in Colorado lived much like the other people who live in the whole Great Plains Culture Area.

The weather on the Plains was very hot in the summer and very cold in the winter. Hard winds, scary tornados, and heavy blizzards blew across the plains. The weather and the soil were not good for farming. The plains were dry and had little rain or snow. The plains in Colorado had only 10-20 inches of rain each year. Plants need water to grow. Often there was not enough water for farming. So, the people who lived on the plains mostly hunted for their food and they gathered wild seeds, berries, and roots. Farming was just too hard.

> **Something to Think About**
>
> If you lived on the Plains of Colorado where there were few trees, how would you make a home for yourself and your family? What resources would you have? Remember, you need to move around a lot to find food in different places. What tools would you need to make your home? Would your shelter be warm in the winter and cool in the summer? Would it be easy to move your home?

Colorado's plains are mostly grassland with only a few willows and cottonwood trees along the rivers and streams. The land is covered in short grass. The Great Plains was the home of the American Bison (buffalo) who grazed on the grasslands. Before

the Europeans came, as many as 60 million buffalo lived on the plains. They are very large, strong animals. Before the Europeans came, the people who lived on the Plains hunted the buffalo on foot and with bows and arrows. They found ways to kill the buffalo for food but it was very dangerous work.

From a drawing by Dario Weilec. Used with permission of the artist.

The coming of the horse changed everything. In about 1630, the Spanish explorers who came to North America brought horses which changed the lifeways of the people. Life on the Plains changed because horses could carry hunters long distances to find game. On horseback, it was possible to follow the herds and the hunts were more successful. It was also possible to leave the women and children safe at home, in one place, while the hunters went far away to hunt. The buffalo provided food, clothing, **tipi** covers, and tools for the people.

There were many Indian tribes that lived on the plains of Colorado. Others came to the Plains to hunt the buffalo. The Cheyenne, Arapaho, Kiowa, Kiowa-Apache, and Comanche lived on the Plains. The Pawnee and Lakota came to hunt, make war, or trade, and are a part of Colorado's history on the Plains.

Tribes, like the Cheyenne and Arapaho, came to the Plains from the East when they were crowded out by the new Europeans. With the horses, they could find enough food to survive on the harsh Plains. Tipis, the homes of the people, were light weight and easy to put up and take down so that families could move to follow the buffalo herds. Horses helped them move their tipis. With horses, they could also travel into the mountains.

Tribes of the Great Plains

■ Cheyenne
■ Arapaho
■ Kiowa
■ Apache
■ Comanche
■ Lakota
■ Pawnee

Tipi

Later, we will explore how the Cheyenne and Arapaho people used the natural resources of the Plains to live happy and peaceful lives.

The Great Basin Culture Area

The mountains and the plateaus of Colorado are located in the Great Basin Culture Area. This large Culture Area is a huge desert basin (like a bowl) with high lands all around it. The Rocky Mountains are on the East side and the Sierra Nevada Mountains are on the West side. Large parts of Utah, Nevada, Wyoming,

> **Major Colorado Mountain Ranges**
>
> ◼ Front Range
> ◼ Sangre de Cristo Range
> ◼ San Juan Mountain Range
> ◼ Sawatch Range
> ◼ Park Range

Idaho, Oregon, California, Colorado, and small parts of Arizona, New Mexico, and Montana are in the Great Basin Culture Area. The Utes along with the Shoshones lived in this Culture Area.

This area has few rivers and not many easy trails to follow. It isn't just one huge basin and there are several mountains ranges and river valleys through the land. The people who lived close to the mountains had more water and game than those who lived in the desert part of the Great Basin.

The people who lived in the Great Basin Area in Colorado would move with the seasons. In the spring and summer they would move to the mountains. They were cool and comfortable in the mountains. There was plenty of game and they would gather foods to store for the winter. In the fall and winter, they moved down from the mountains to the plateaus. They settled in the canyons and other places where they would be protected from the winter weather. They lived where they could find firewood and water easily. They hoped that the food they had stored for winter would last until spring. In the spring they would move back to the mountains. This kind of travel is called a "**seasonal round**." Sometimes the people would plant corn, beans, and squash in the spring

and hope that there would be some crops when they returned in the fall.

The mountains also had valuable resources hidden under the ground. Gold, silver, coal, and other minerals were discovered in Colorado by the settlers. The Indians lived on the land as they found it and didn't care much about these minerals. The settlers treasured them. In their world, these resources could make them rich. In today's time, other valuable resources like natural gas have been found underground. But, that's a story for later.

The plateaus of Colorado are a part of the Great Basin Culture Area. They are high, flat areas often with one or more very steep sides or cliffs. There are flat **mesas** and deep canyons in the plateaus. The temperature and precipitation of the plateaus are affected by the mountains and their elevation. Days can be hot and the nights cold.

Grand Mesa, Colorado—the biggest mesa in the world

The Plateaus are very dry also. You will see sagebrush and piñon and juniper trees in the mountains and on the plateaus. Indian people who lived in the plateaus spent most of their time hunting for food. They hunted for rabbits, snakes, lizards, and birds. They gathered seeds, nuts, berries, roots, and insects. Their homes called **wickiups** were scattered all through the area. Families lived alone or in small groups, always moving to find what they needed to survive.

The Southwest Culture Area

The Southwest Culture area is a large area in North America. It covers almost all of Arizona and New Mexico and a very large part of Mexico.

Tribes of the Great Basin and Southwest

- Ute
- Shoshone
- Pueblo groups
- Navajo
- Apache

Just some small edges of this culture area are in Colorado. This area has mountains, plateaus, and deserts. All of this area is dry.

Wickiup

Less than 20 inches of rain to less than 4 inches of rain falls in this area each year. In the early times, the people mostly lived in grass-covered wik-iups or in earth-covered hogans. Because there was so little rain, there also were fewer animals for food and hides. Farming was hard but some people learned how to save water and to irrigate their crops.There were also people who did **Hogan** not stay in one place. They mostly hunted and gathered their food. Some Ancient Pueblo and the Fremont people probably lived in this area.

How Should The Land Be Used?

After the settlers came to Colorado they used the land, rivers, plants, and animals in different ways than the Indians. The Indians believed the land and its resources were **sacred**. They called the land Mother Earth. The settlers believed that the land should be used to make money. These different beliefs caused very danger-ous and hard times for the Indian people in Colorado.

Indian people believed that the earth is their mother and a gift from the **Creator**. Mother Earth takes care of them. She provides all that they need for food, for clothing, and for shelter. The earth provides medicines for when they are sick or hurt. Mother Earth also provides resources for tools and ways to make travel easier. Indian people knew that they must take loving care of their mother who provided for them.

Indian people also believed that the land was to be used by everyone for their survival. No one person owned the land. There were no laws that kept other people from the land. This was especially important for tribes that had to move with the seasons of the year.

The Indians believed that they should use the land and the natural resources carefully. They took only what they needed. Balance was kept between nature and the land. When they killed an animal

Something to Think About

Imagine that you were Grace's great, great, great grandfather. Your family has two boys and a baby girl. Your grandmother lives with your family, too. That makes six people to feed, clothe, and keep warm and safe. You are a proud hunter. Your family always has enough food. The buffalo gives you meat to eat. Their bones were made into tools like spoons, scrapping tools, shields, and containers for water. You use the hides for blankets, tipi covers, and leather for clothing and moccasins. You are grateful for the buffalo that the Creator gave to you.

Then, one day railroad tracks are built across your hunting grounds. The train engines belch terrible black smoke and make loud and strange noises They frighten the buffalo from this land. Now, it is hard for you to find buffalo and your family is very hungry. Winter is coming. How do you feel about trains and railroad tracks? Do you respect the men who brought them across your land? Should you try to stop the railroads?

Now, imagine that you are a business man from the East who is building a railroad to Colorado. You know that there are many people going west to find gold and silver. There are others who want to build towns with homes, schools, churches, and businesses. Some want to build large cattle and sheep ranches. They need to get important supplies from the East. They also need to get the animal furs that they trap, the cattle they raise, and the crops they grow to the East where people will buy them. A railroad provides fast and safe transportation for the settlers. A railroad joins the country from East to West and makes communication easier. It helps people to settle the West and build the country. It will also make a lot of money for your business.

The land is open and no one owns it. How do you feel about the Indians who are making it dangerous to build a railroad? Some of them are attacking the trains. Should you stop building the railroad?

It's easy to see that these different beliefs are going to cause problems! How could these problems be solved?

The Ute Mountain Utes believe that The Sleeping Ute Mountains are sacred. This mountain range in southern Colorado looks like a Ute Chief lying on his back with arms folded across his chest. The legend of the Sleeping Ute tells why the mountains are important to the Ute people. The legend and the sacred Sleeping Ute Mountains are still a part of their ceremonies today. Use the Internet to learn more about the Sleeping Ute.

for food, they thanked the animal for giving its life to feed their families. They took special care not to kill the mothers and young animals because they needed the herd to keep growing. They used every part of the animal and didn't waste anything. Animals were their relatives and treated with respect.

The European and American farmers, ranchers, miners, settlers, traders, and trappers had very different beliefs about the land. They believed that it should be used for different reasons.

The Europeans and Americans believed that the land was to be used to make money. Mining, grazing, and harvesting of trees and crops gave them the most money in the shortest time. They didn't look ahead to the future. They didn't think about what would happen when they chopped down all the trees to build homes and make firewood for new towns. They didn't understand that when all the beaver are trapped, they would be **extinct**. They didn't care that when all the buffalo are killed, people would starve. And, they didn't remember that when the rivers are polluted, the fish would die.

They also believed that since no one owned the land, they had a right to claim it as their land. They could farm and ranch and bring in cattle, sheep, and fences. They could build towns, churches, stores, mines and railroads anywhere. They believed that the Indians were savages that kept them from using the land. They thought that the Indians didn't really own or use the land in the right way.

For thousands of years, the Mountains, Plains, and Plateaus of Colorado supported Indian people. Then the European and American settlers came. The settlers brought new ways and beliefs about the land and its resources. As you learn about the traditional ways and beliefs of the Utes, the Cheyenne, and the Arapaho, and about the changes brought by the settlers you will understand why there was big trouble ahead.

More Books to Read

Bruchac, Joseph. *The Circle of Thanks: Native American Poems and Songs of Thanksgiving.* Mahwah, NJ: BridgeWater, 1996.

Goble, Paul. *Death of the Iron Horse.* New York, NY: Bradbury, 1987.

Swamp, Chief Jake *Giving Thanks: A Native American Good Morning Message.* New York, NY: Lee & Low, 1995.

Places to Go

Plains Conservation Center

21901 E. Hampden Ave.
Aurora, CO 80014
Phone: 303-693-3621

Websites to Visit

Physical maps of Colorado: http://fermi.jhuapl.edu/states/states.html

Plains Conservation Center: http://www.plainsconservationcenter.org

Maps to Look At

Waldman, Carl. *Atlas of the North American Indian.* New York, NY: Checkmark/Facts on File. 2000.

Noble, David Grant. *Ancient Colorado: An Archaeological Perspective.* Denver, CO: Colorado Council of Professional Archaeologists, 2000.

Things to Do

Elevation/Temperature/Precipitation

Find a weather map in the newspaper. Which cities have the highest temperatures? Which cities have the lowest temperatures? What makes the difference? What cities have the most precipitation? What cities have the least precipitation? What makes the difference?

Where Do You Live?

Locate where you live on a map. Do you live in the Great Plains Culture Area, or The Great Basin Culture Area? Do you live in the mountains or the plateaus? Choose five words that describe your environment.

Find The Population of These Colorado Cities

■ Denver
■ Colorado Springs

■ Greeley
■ Fort Collins
■ Pueblo
■ Gunnison
■ Durango
■ Grand Junction

Colorado Rivers

On a map of Colorado, draw these rivers in Colorado. Why were rivers important to the Indians?

■ South Platte River
■ Republican River
■ Arkansas River
■ Rio Grande River
■ Gunnison River
■ Colorado River

Popcorn?

Popcorn is an ancient food in the Americas. Do you think the Indians in Colorado grew popcorn? Check out this website: http://www.popcorn.org

Mother Earth

Simon Ortiz said this:

> *The Earth is the source of all life.*
> *She gives birth.*
> *Her children continue the life of the earth.*
> *The People must be responsible to her.*
> *This is the way that all life continues.*

Ortiz, Simon. The People Shall Continue (Rev.). *San Francisco, CA: Children's Book Press, p. 3,. 1988.*

What does Simon Ortiz ask us to do? Why? List 5 ways you can be responsible to Mother Earth.

Make a Relief Map

Materials you will need:

A flat piece of heavy cardboard (such as the side of a heavy cardboard box), a very large pizza box, or a thin, square piece of wood, large mixing bowl, measuring cup; pencil, watercolors, poster paints, or food coloring, paint brushes, road map, the list of required items, and lots of time and patience.

Recipe:
1 cup of table salt

2 cups of flour (use all-purpose flour, not self-rising flour)

1 cup of water

Directions:
1. In pencil, draw or trace an outline of Colorado on your cardboard or piece of wood.

2. Mix the salt, flour, and water in a large bowl until smooth and pliable (like cookie dough, not runny like cake batter). You might need to add more water or flour and salt to get the right consistency. You might also need to double or triple this recipe, depending on the size of your map.

3. Spread a thin layer of the mixture within the outline of Colorado, trimming any excess.

4. Refer to your state map. With your hands, use more mixture to form the elevated regions (Mountains, Plains, and Plateaus).

5. Form the rivers with a pencil or knife.

6. Set your relief map aside in a safe place to dry. The drying time will depend on how thick your mixture is and the weather. Your map must dry naturally. If you try to speed up the drying process in any way, such as putting it in an oven or using a hair dryer, it is extremely likely to crack and you will have to start over. After your map is dry, make a map legend.

7. Paint your map according to your legend and locate and label the landforms on your map.

8. *Be creative and have fun as you learn about our state!*

Match the Culture Area to the Homes

Culture Area	Kinds of Homes
Northeast	Skins
Arctic	Wood and Bark
Plains	Ice and Snow

Something to think about

Do you think the Sleeping Ute Mountains would be a good place to develop a big ski resort? Explalin your answer.

Definitions

Basin	a land form that is shaped like a bowl
Climate	type of weather found in an area
Creator	name given to the spirit or God that people worshipped
Culture Areas	name scientists gave to environments that were much alike
Elevation	how high or low the land is compared to sea level
Environment	the climate, landforms, and natural resources that surround us
Extinct	no longer exists
Landforms	the shape and features of the land - mountains, plains, plateaus, basins, oceans, and rivers
Mesa	a raised area of land with a flat top and steep sides
Mountain	a natural raised part of the earth larger than a hill
Natural Resources	those things in nature that people use such as trees, plants, animals, soil, and water
Permanent	stays the same or in the same place
Plain	a big open area of flat land
Plateau	an area of high flat land surrounded by one or more mountains
Precipitation	rain, snow, or any other kind of moisture that falls from the sky
Survive	to live and not die
Sacred	something that is worthy of great honor and respect
Seasonal Round	when people follow the seasons to find food and come back to the same places each year
Tipi	a home shaped like a cone which is made with logs and covered with hides
Wickiup	temporary camp shelters that were used before and shortly after the Ute obtained the horse.

Thanks to Mother Earth

*Onen, we give thanks
to our mother, the Earth,
for she gives us all that we need for life.*

*She supports our feet as we walk upon her.
She is there to catch us
if we should fall.*

*It has always been this way
since the beginning,
for she is our mother
the one who cares for us.*

*It gives us great joy
that Mother Earth
continues still to care for us.*

*So it is that we join
our minds together
to give greetings and thanks
to this Earth, our mother.*

Bruchac, Joseph. The Circle of Thanks: Native American Poems and Songs of Thanksgiving. *Mahwah, NH: BridgeWater. 1996.*

Chapter 3
The Old Ones: The Ancient Puebloans

There is so much excitement in the air. This is the day for the fifth grade field trip. The sun is bright and the sky is blue. It's a beautiful Colorado morning! With her loaded backpack and new sleeping bag, Grace is really excited. Her friends, their teachers, and some moms and dads are ready to get on the yellow school bus. Everyone is waving and saying goodbye. "Have a great time!" "Don't forget your coat!" "Remember your camera!" " Bye, Mom."

Grace's fifth grade class raised the money for this field trip. They had bake sales and car washes and did chores at home to earn money. Their parents helped and they all worked hard. Now they are going all the way across Colorado to visit **Mesa Verde** National Park. They have been studying about the **prehistoric** people who lived there. Now, they will see where they actually lived.

Quickly they will drive through the mountains, across the parks, and into a land of plateaus and mesas, cliffs, canyons, and deserts. It's a long drive to the **Four Corners**. Grace's mother packed some apples, cookies, and other snacks to enjoy and share. She also put a new book, Race to the Moonrise, into her backpack to read on the bus. It's a story about very long ago in the desert Southwest. Grace is ready to ride across Colorado!

Mesa Verde is just a short drive from Durango, Colorado. The school bus moves quickly along the highway from Durango to Cortez. Grace is excited and tired too. She looks out the window and watches how the environment is changing. It is starting to look very different from Denver. As they drive out of Durango, the mountains seem to be behind them. The land begins to look more flat and dry. There are fewer and fewer houses.

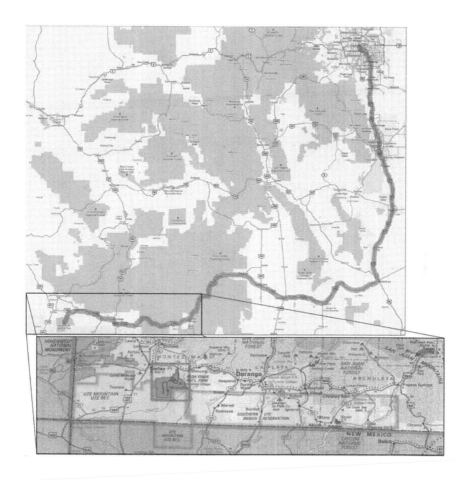

They are entering the plateaus and desert where the Great Basin Culture Area and the Southwest Culture meet. Grace is about to take her first step backward into the lives of the Old Ones. They are some of the first Indian people to live in Colorado.

The Old Ones used to be known as the Anasazi. That was the name that was given to them by the Navajo people. It means "ancient ones " or "enemy ancestors" in the Navajo language. Now the Old Ones are called Ancient Puebloans. They are the ancient ancestors of the Pueblo people, including the Hopi and Zuni and others who live along the Rio Grande River in Arizona and New Mexico. They lived in the Four Corners area from approximately

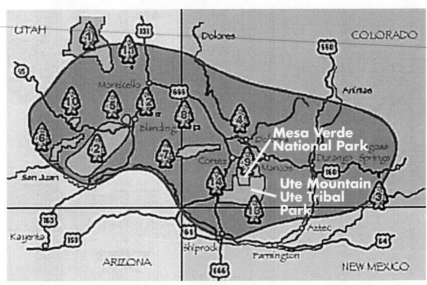

Archeological sites in the Four Corners area

550 A.D. to 1300 A.D. That means that they lived in Colorado about 700 years. Then, they disappeared mysteriously.

How do we know about the lives of people who lived so long ago? There is no written history to tell us. There are no people who are alive now to tell us their stories and show us their homes and their dances. There are several ways we learn about the past. The first way, is by digging and analyzing.

Imagine that a stranger came to your house every week for a month and took everything that was in your wastepaper baskets, your recycling bins, and your trash cans. They took all this trash and garbage from your house and stored it in a huge pit. Then, they forgot all about it. One hundred or one thousand years later, scientists called **archaeologists** found this pit. They began to dig up and look through your trash to find out about how your family lived long ago.

Each little piece of your trash was a clue. Some of the trash had decayed. Some was broken. Some of it wasn't even your trash! It certainly didn't tell everything about your family. But, little bit by little bit, they began to learn something about how you lived. Their ideas are usually right. But sometimes their ideas were wrong too.

Archaeologists have problems when they are learning about people of long ago. First, they can't say that all people in the community lived exactly alike because families are different. Also, some of the things about every family are very special. These special things can't go in the trash. They are feelings like love and caring. They are ideas like beliefs and values. They are traditions and special activities that families do together. Scientists will never know everything about families of long ago and their ancient cultures.

Digging and studying is one way archaeologists work. They discover what ancient people left behind in their trash and in their homes. Then they try to figure out how they lived long ago. All kinds of technology help them. Every year new tools are developed that make their work easier and more accurate. Remember that it's hard to know anything for sure. No one was there thousands of years ago and often what makes people special isn't the things they have. It is what they believe and think that is important.

Another way to learn about the lifeways of the Ancient Puebloans is by learning about their **descendants**. Today's Pueblo people are their descendants. Scientists learn as much as they can about the lifeways, beliefs, traditions, and stories that have been passed on to them by their ancestors. These ways of life probably started with the people we know as the Ancient Puebloans. When we learn about today's Pueblo people, we are also learning something about their ancestors. However, there are many stories and ceremonies that the Pueblo people don't talk about to other people. So, we still don't know everything about them. But learning as much as we can about the lifeways and beliefs of today's Pueblos is a very important part of how we know about the Old Ones.

Mesa Verde

A mesa is a high landform that has a flat top and steep sides. Mesa means "table" in Spanish and verde means "green." The sides of the mesa have caves, ledges, and rock overhangs. The first people to live here lived on top of the mesas. Later, people built homes and communities in the cliffs. The people were farmers and planted their crops on the mesas.

Pit House

Like all cultures, the Ancient Puebloans changed over time. The earliest people were called the "Basketmakers." They lived in pit houses on the tops of the mesas. Their crops were stored in pits plastered with clay and covered in stone. Then, they began to make houses above ground with logs, sticks, and mud.

Later, they moved from these comfortable homes on top of the mesas into the cliffs. Their new homes were made of stone and mud or **adobe** bricks. The roofs were made with logs with sticks, grasses, and mud on the top. These homes were called pueblos.

Pueblo

"Pueblo" is the Spanish word for village. The pueblos were joined together to form a community. The small communities came together to make larger communities.

These homes were as high as four or even five stories with many rooms. They were very hard to reach which protected them from their enemies. The people climbed up to their homes on ladders or they made hand and foot holds in the walls. Climbing to your

The parts of a kiva

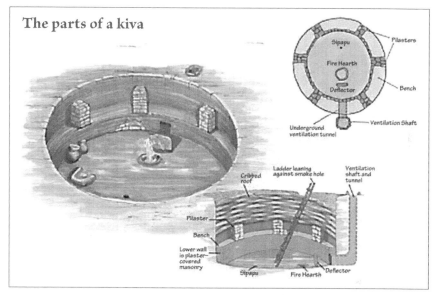

home was very dangerous! In some places they had tunnels to crawl through to reach their homes. The rooms had very small windows and doors to keep them warm in the winter.

Round rooms called "kivas" were dug into the ground. The men would gather in the kivas for special ceremonies.

A modern kiva in New Mexico

Cliff Palace

Sometimes they were used by all the people for other activities, especially in the winter because the kivas were warmer than their homes.

Cliff Palace is the largest dwelling at Mesa Verde. It has 271 rooms and 23 kivas. The rooms are very small and not very high. They don't have many windows. Water usually had to be carried to the cliff homes. We know much about the people who lived at Cliff Palace because they threw their trash in the front of the cliff.

The people were very busy getting water, growing, preparing, and storing food, and making clothes. They grew beans, corn, and squash on the mesas and in the valleys. They also hunted elk, antelope, deer, big horned sheep, and small animals like rabbits and prairie dogs. From the forests, they gathered wood to build homes and make fires and nuts to eat. Fish and ducks were caught. Berries and seeds were gathered from the valleys. They had dogs and turkeys. The turkeys were used for food and their feathers were woven into blankets.

Mano and metate

Each home had a fire pit and cooking utensils. The people would set their cooking pots on three stones on the hearth. They also had flat stone griddles that they used to bake flat piki bread. Piki bread looked like tortillas. They baked corn and other food in ovens they dug in the earth and covered with stones. The women made clay pots to hold water, store grains, and cook food. The corn was ground by the women with manos and metates. A **metate** is a large, flat stone. The corn, seeds, or nuts were put on the metate and ground into meal using a small hand stone, or **mano**. Mush or piki bread was made with ground corn.

Where is the Dentist?

Cornmeal was eaten at nearly every meal. When corn was ground with a mano and metate, there would be small bits of grit in the cornmeal. When people ate the cornmeal, it would slowly grind down their teeth. Many people had problems with their teeth.

In the summer, people didn't wear many clothes, just aprons around their waists. In the cold winters they wore robes and and blankets that were made of rabbit skins or woven from cotton and turkey feathers. Shirts, pants, and moccasins were made from deer skin. They had to trade with people from the south to get cotton for weaving. Shawls and blankets were also woven with animal hair and

Ancient Puebloan pottery from Mesa Verde

turkey feathers and cotton. Sandals were woven with yucca.

There were no horses at Mesa Verde. People traveled by foot. Some of the roads that they used can still be found today.

The people created many beautiful things. The men and women wore lovely jewelry decorated with turquoise. The women made baskets and covered them with pitch

Petroglyphs

from the piñon trees to make them waterproof. Clay was collected to make beautiful pottery that was decorated with paints made with natural materials. Some pottery was decorated by pinching the clay. Because these pots were rough on the outside, they were easier to carry. People also made beautiful pictures called petroglyphs and pictographs on the rocks.

Now, the mystery part. No one knows for sure why the Old Ones left the Four Corners area. In about 1280 A.D. people started to leave Mesa Verde and move south. By 1300 the Old Ones had left Mesa Verde. Scientists don't know why they left, but here are some possible reasons:

- ■ After a long **drought** from 1276 to 1297, there was not enough food or water.
- ■ There were so many people that they could not feed everyone.
- ■ Enemies drove them out.
- ■ A terrible disease killed nearly everyone.
- ■ They left for religious reasons.
- ■ There was so much war, that they moved to a place that was more peaceful.

Why do you think the Old Ones left Mesa Verde?

The Trader is Coming: A Story

The night sky was getting lighter and the stars were beginning to fade away. It was still very quiet in the village. Turquoise Girl was just beginning to wake up. Her world was beginning to wake up too. Her eyes were still closed but she could hear soft sounds of the turkeys. Her nose could smell the smoke of a new fire in the plaza. She opened her eyes and pulled her warm turkey feather blanket close around her. The morning was chilly. Winter would be coming soon. Her grandmother was building a large fire outside and starting to cook the morning meal of corn cakes for her family.

Turquoise Girl wanted to stay wrapped in her blanket as long as she could. She shared her room with Raven, her brother. It was a small room. But, it was comfortable. Some blankets and clothes were stored in the room too. Soon Mother would come to wake them up. They could sleep a little longer today. They had just returned from the Harvest Festival and were still a little tired from the travel and the excitement. Turquoise Girl was thinking of the wonderful Harvest Festival and the winter that would be coming soon.

The crops of corn, beans, and squash were very good this year. Father had done most of the planting on the mesa with his digging stick. Turquoise Girl and Raven helped put some of the red, black, blue, yellow, and speckled corn seeds in the the holes. They also helped keep the birds, rabbits, deer and bugs away from the crops. The Cloud People sent rain clouds in the summer to water the crops and they grew well. Turquoise Girl, Raven, and most of the people in the village helped to gather the crops in the fall. They filled their storerooms with food for the winter. The corn was stored in beautiful clay pots.

The Harvest Festival was held after all the crops were harvested. All of the people in the village walked to the Great Kiva in the large village to the south. Just the small babies and the elders stayed at home. People from other villages joined them. Everyone traveled together to thank the Cloud People and to celebrate the successful harvest. Women from the villages chose perfect ears of corn, Corn Mothers, for the dancers to carry. The men tied prayer feathers around the Corn Mothers.

Turquoise Girl's family stayed with relatives while the men entered the large kiva to get ready to dance. It was good to visit with friends and relatives. They all came to the Great Kiva to thank the Cloud People for the rain that made the crops grow. The dancers wore beautiful clothes as they came slowly out of the kiva. They spread cornmeal ahead of them as they began to dance. They danced the ancient sacred dance of thanksgiving and then returned to the kiva. They did this three times. The chanting and drumming sounded like the heartbeat of the earth. The dancers thanked the Cloud People for the good harvest. There was much food stored for the winter!

When the dance was over, it was time to start the journey home. On the way home from the Harvest Festival, her family stopped along the way to gather more piñon nuts. They arrived home, happy, safe, and tired.

Turquoise Girl thought about the work that she needed to do the next morning. With her friends, she would grind corn like she did every morning. But she also thought of the trader's visit and the things they needed for winter. When her family was at the central kiva they learned that the trader was on his way to the village. Everyone would be getting ready for the trader's visit. There was much work to do to prepare for him.

The trader would bring cotton for weaving from the south, some beautiful turquoise for carving, some salt for cooking, and maybe some shells and feathers or copper bells. Sometimes, he brought some colorful feathers of the macaw. He also brought news of other villages. Turquoise Girl's father was hoping he would bring some special rocks that would make strong tools.

Her family needed to have things ready to trade. Mother had made a pretty pot with black and white designs. Grandmother had made a yucca basket. Father had made a long necklace with many beads of turquoise. Grandfather had tanned deer skin and Grandmother had sewn them into soft leggings. Turquoise Girl had nothing to trade. She was still learning to make pots from Grandmother. Maybe she would have a lovely pot for the trader's next visit. But what could she do to welcome the trader who would be coming in a few days?

Then she had a wonderful idea. Her family would prepare a special meal to honor the trader. They would have roasted deer meat, beans, squash, and sweet corn cakes. When she ground the corn this morning, she would make enough ground corn to make sweet corn cakes for the trader's dinner. Sweet corn cakes were very special. She would sing corn songs with her friends. Then she would chew some corn meal. When the cornmeal is chewed, the saliva (spit) changes the corn's starch to sugar. This is mixed with the other cornmeal. Then the meal is formed into balls and dropped into a pot of boiling water. Sweet corn cakes are a special food that is made for honored guests. The trader will know that he is welcome in the village.

It will be a good visit and many trades will be made. The village will have new supplies from other villages to work on during the cold winter days. They will have cotton, turquoise, salt, and other treasures from far away. The cold winter days will pass quickly. The storerooms are filled with food. The people will be busy making warm blankets, beautiful jewelry, and strong baskets. There will be storytelling and warm fires in the kiva too! Then it will be time to begin to sprout the beans to plant in the spring.

Other Ancient People in Colorado

The Ancient Puebloans were not Grace's ancestors. But archaeologists are making new discoveries all the time. In November 2004, archaeologists were working at a building site in Parker, Colorado when they uncovered evidence of peo-

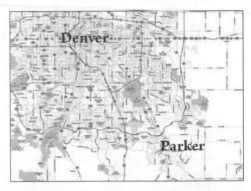

ple who lived there about 5,000 years ago. Their homes were built near a stream in what is now the town of Parker which is close to Denver. This was not a temporary camp. The houses were large and nearly 24 feet across. They were made with wood posts and walls of brush or animal hides. Fire pits were in the centers of the homes and there were storage pits for food.

The scientists found butchered bison bones, spear points, and pit houses. A stone circle was found that might have been used for ceremonies. The people hunted and gathered seeds and berries for food. They probably moved often, following the game. Then, they must have returned to the homes they had built.

It isn't known if today's tribes were related to these people. While they are studying this new discovery, the scientists will respect other tribal traditions. This discovery will help archaeologists understand a period of time that they don't know much about. Who knows, maybe they were Grace's ancestors!

Little is known about the **Apishapa** people, who lived in southeastern Colorado home 1,000 years ago. They may be the ancestors of some of the Southeastern Plains Indians. The Apishapa were a hunting and gathering people who followed a seasonal round. They stayed for along time in one place before moving with the seasons to find food and game. Then they would return. Archaeologists think they may have returned to the same locations for hundred of years.

Their homes were made with rocks placed in a circle as a base to the home. Then posts and brush, and mud were added to make the rest of the home. They usually were single homes, but sometimes they were connected to make larger homes with many rooms. Their homes have been found hidden on canyon rims, or tucked into the rocks. They had good sources of water and their homes were built where they could see the land around them which made them more safe.

These people ate seeds, berries, roots and other parts of plants and stored them to use in the winter. Some corn has been found, so they probably did some farming or traded for corn. They also made stone tools with stone found around them or they traded with others far away for other kinds of stone. They made tools for cutting, scraping, drilling, grinding, and hunting. **Sherds** from large gray jars and small bone beads have been found. An exhibit at the Colorado Historical Museum shows how scientists believe these people lived.

The **Fremont** people lived north of the Ancient Puebloans. They lived in pit houses, wickiups, and shelters in the rocks. Mostly they gathered their food like piñon nuts, rice grass, and rabbits, birds, and fish. About 650 A.D. they left their settlements and lived a more nomadic life, searching for food. They were probably the ancestors of today's Ute people.

These people, the Ancient Puebloans, the Apishapa, the Fremont, and perhaps others that we don't know much about yet, were some of the first Indian people to live in Colorado. While some moved to other places, other Indian people came to Colorado later. Now, let's go forward to learn about the Utes who have always lived here.

The Ancient People of the Four Corners: A Timeline

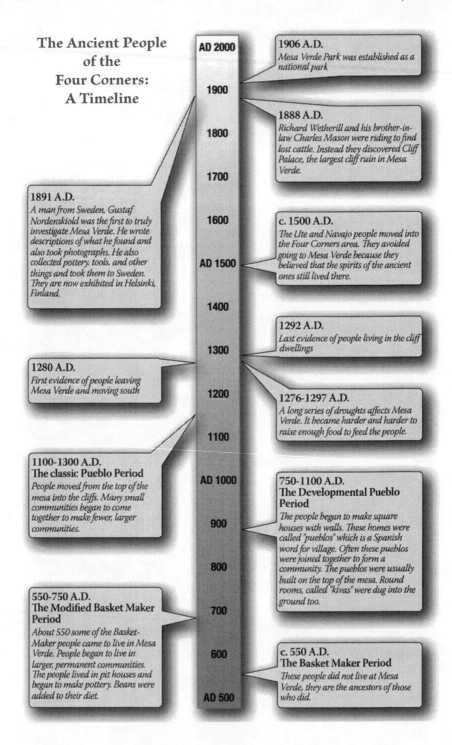

AD 2000

1900

1800

1700

1600

AD 1500

1400

1300

1200

1100

AD 1000

900

800

700

600

AD 500

1906 A.D.
Mesa Verde Park was established as a national park

1888 A.D.
Richard Wetherill and his brother-in-law Charles Mason were riding to find lost cattle. Instead they discovered Cliff Palace, the largest cliff ruin in Mesa Verde.

1891 A.D.
A man from Sweden, Gustaf Nordenskiold was the first to truly investigate Mesa Verde. He wrote descriptions of what he found and also took photographs. He also collected pottery, tools, and other things and took them to Sweden. They are now exhibited in Helsinki, Finland.

c. 1500 A.D.
The Ute and Navajo people moved into the Four Corners area. They avoided going to Mesa Verde because they believed that the spirits of the ancient ones still lived there.

1292 A.D.
Last evidence of people living in the cliff dwellings

1280 A.D.
First evidence of people leaving Mesa Verde and moving south

1276-1297 A.D.
A long series of droughts affects Mesa Verde. It became harder and harder to raise enough food to feed the people.

1100-1300 A.D.
The classic Pueblo Period
People moved from the top of the mesa into the cliffs. Many small communities began to come together to make fewer, larger communities.

750-1100 A.D.
The Developmental Pueblo Period
The people began to make square houses with walls. These homes were called "pueblos" which is a Spanish word for village. Often these pueblos were joined together to form a community. The pueblos were usually built on the top of the mesa. Round rooms, called "kivas" were dug into the ground too.

550-750 A.D.
The Modified Basket Maker Period
About 550 some of the Basket-Maker people came to live in Mesa Verde. People began to live in larger, permanent communities. The people lived in pit houses and began to make pottery. Beans were added to their diet.

c. 550 A.D.
The Basket Maker Period
These people did not live at Mesa Verde, they are the ancestors of those who did.

More Books to Read

Arnold, Caroline. *The Ancient Cliff Dwellers of Mesa Verde.* New York, NY: Clarion, 1992.

Creel, Ann Howard. *Under a Stand Still Moon.* Weston, CT: Brown Barn Books 2005.

Crumb, Sally. *Race to the Moonrise: An Ancient Journey.* Ouray, CO: Western Reflections 1998.

Shuter, Jane. *Visiting the Past: Mesa Verde.* Chicago, IL: Heinemann Library, 2000.

Skurzynski, Gloria., and Alane Ferguson. *Cliff-hanger.* New York, NY: Scholastic, 1999.

Young, Robert. *A Personal Tour of Mesa Verde.* Minneapolis, MN: Lerner, 1999.

Videos to Watch

Mesa Verde National Park: Legacy of Stone and Spirit. [Video]. New Dimension Media. (48 minutes), 1997.

Places to Go

Anasazi Heritage Center
27501 Highway 184
Dolores, CO 81323
Phone: 970-882-5600

Colorado Historical Society (Ancient Voices: Stories of Colorado's Distant Past)
1300 Broadway
Denver, CO 80203
Phone: 303-866-3682

Mesa Verde National Park
P.O. Box 8
Mesa Verde National Park, CO 81330

Ute Mountain Ute Tribal Park
P.O. Box 109
Towaoc, CO 81334
Phone: 1-800-847-5485

Websites to Visit

Anasazi Heritage Center http://www.co blm.gov/ahd/index.htm

Colorado Historical Society http://www.coloradohistory.org

Mesa Verde National Park http://www.nps.gov/meve/

Ute Mountain Ute Tribal Park
        http://www.utemountainute.com/tribalpark.htm

Things to Do

How Big was Turquoise Girl's Room?

The room that Turquoise Girl's room slept in was about eight feet long, six feet wide, and five and one-half feet high. On the floor or ground, use masking tape or chalk to show the size of a room in a cliff dwelling.

Make a Petroglyph

What You Need:

- ■ Plaster of Paris
- ■ Water
- ■ Container for mixing plaster
- ■ Stick or spoon for mixing plaster
- ■ Flat, plastic lid from coffee can
- ■ Paper clip (optional)
- ■ Carving tools (pencil, old ball-point pen, stick, or sharp stone)
- ■ Paint or shoe polish
- ■ Acrylic floor wax.

What To Do:

Mix the plaster and water following the directions on the plaster package. When it begins to thicken, pour some onto the lid until it's covered. If you want to hang your petroglyph on the wall, push a paper clip into the plaster before it hardens. Later you can hang it from a nail. Let the plaster harden, and then peel away the lid. Use your carving tool to scratch a picture of design in the plaster. Paint the plaster or rub shoe polish over it with a cloth rag. Brush on a coat of acrylic floor wax to give it a shiny finish. Use designs that the **Ancient Puebloans** might have used.

SOURCE: Carlson, Laurie. 1994. More Than Moccasins. Chicago, IL: Chicago Review Press. pp. 164-165.

Make Hopi Blue Marbles

This recipe is a new version of the way the Hopi people used to make "blue marbles." The Hopi are **descendants** of the Ancestral Puebloans. Modern ingredients are used in this recipe. If you do not use blue corn meal, you can add blue food coloring.

What You Need:

1 cup of finely ground blue cornmeal

1 teaspoon baking powder

2 tablespoons of sugar

4 drops of blue food coloring (optional)

3/4 cup of boiling water.

What To Do:

Mix the cornmeal, baking powder, and sugar. Stir the food coloring into the boiling water. Stir into the cornmeal mixture, a tablespoonful at a time. Add only enough water so that the dough holds together. Roll small pieces of the dough into balls the size of marbles. Heat 4 cups of water to a gentle simmer in a heavy, wide-mouthed saucepan. Drop in the cornmeal balls and simmer gently, uncovered, for 10 minutes. Ladle the marbles and some cooking liquid into small bowls and serve at once.

Definitions

Adobe	a brick or building material of sun-dried earth and straw
Ancestor	a family member that lived a long time ago
Ancient Puebloans	the more accurate name that has replaced "Anasazi" for the people of Mesa Verde who were the ancestors of today's Pueblo people
Ancient	old or from a long time ago
Apishapa	an ancient people who lived in Southeastern Colorado
Archaeologists	scientists who study of any prehistoric culture by digging and studying the **artifacts** that they find
Artifact	any object used or made by a human being
Descendants	the members of the family that were born after them; their children, grandchildren, great-grandchildren and so on.

Desert Culture	the people who lived west of the plains in the mountains, foothills, and plateau areas around the Colorado river as early as 7000 B. C.
Drought	a very long period where there is no rainfall for the crops
Four Corners	the area around the place where New Mexico, Arizona, Utah, and Colorado meet
Lifeways	the ways people live—their homes, foods, clothing, families, arts and crafts, laws and leaders, trade, beliefs and values, and traditions
Mano	a stone that grinds corn on a metate
Mesa Verde	a high plateau in southwestern Colorado that was the home of the Ancient Puebloans
Metate	a flat stone with high sides; a mano is used to grind corn and meat on a metate
Prehistoric	The time before history was written down
Sherds	(also, potsherds or shards) pieces of ancient pottery
Sipapu	a Hopi word for a small hole in the floor of kivas. It is a reminder of the opening through which the ancient ancestors first emerged to enter the present world.

Chapter 4
Ute Life in the Past

Grace is proud to be Southern Cheyenne. Her Grandmother tells her stories about her Southern Cheyenne ancestors of long ago. In the past, they were enemies of the Ute. They often fought over buffalo hunting territories. The Ute people had different ways of life than the Cheyenne. They had their own beliefs, values, and lifeways.

Long ago, almost all of the western part of Colorado belonged to the Utes. They were the people who lived in the mountains, plateaus, and deserts of the Great Basin Culture Area. Were they living there at the same time as the Ancient Puebloans? How did the people of the mountains, plateaus, and deserts live? Col-

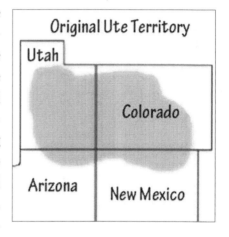

orado's mountains are high and the plateaus are very dry. Grace knows it would be cold and dangerous to live in Colorado's mountains in the winter. How were the lifeways of the Utes in the Great Basin different from the lifeways of the Cheyenne on the Plains?

Grace is right about living in the Great Basin! These lands have tall mountains, high plateaus, and dry deserts. The Utes had the same needs for food, clothing, and shelter as the Cheyenne. But, they lived in a different environment and had different natural resources to meet those needs.

The Ute Indians have lived in Colorado longer than any other people. They called themselves "Nuche." This means, "The People." Long ago other Indian people called them "People of the

Shining Mountains." They have a story that tells them how they came to live here. This is called a creation story.

The earliest Utes may have arrived in Colorado from California and Utah. They probably came about five hundred to eight hundred years ago. Some Utes believe that the ancient Fremont people were some of their ancestors. There are also some people who believe that the Utes might have pushed the Ancient Puebloans into the safety of their homes in the cliffs!

If the Utes tried to go out of their mountains, other Indian groups would fight to drive them back. The other tribes wanted to protect their hunting lands on the plains. So the Utes stayed near their shining mountains and they were a peaceful people.

Long ago, there were seven bands of Utes that lived in Colorado. Two bands, the Mouache and Capote, are now the present day Southern Utes. Today, their headquarters are

Creation Story: How the Utes Came to Be

Long ago, even before the ancient times, only Sinawav, the Creator, and Coyote lived on the earth. The earth was young. It was time to have people. Sinawav gave a bag of sticks to Coyote. Then he said, "Carry these over the far hills to the valleys beyond." He told Coyote where to go and what to do. He said, "Coyote, this is a great responsibility. The bag must never be opened until you reach the sacred grounds."

"What is this I carry?" asked Coyote.

"I will say no more. Now do your task," Sinawav answered.

Coyote was foolish and very curious. "What is this I carry?" he kept asking himself. As soon as he was over the first hill, he stopped. He was just going to peek in the bag. "That won't hurt anything," he thought. Just as he untied the bag, people rushed to get out.

These people spoke in strange languages. He tried to catch them and get them back into the bag. But they ran away in all different directions. The bag was almost empty. There were only a few people left. So, he went to the sacred valley and dumped them out. Those few people were the Utes, the real Utes. Coyote then went back and told Sinawav that he had finished the job.

Sinawav looked at Coyote's face. "I know," Sinawav sighed. "You foolish thing. You do not know what a bad thing you have done."

Coyote finally told the truth. "I tried to catch them. I was scared. They spoke in strange languages that I couldn't understand."

"The people that you let escape will always fight with the Utes. They will be the tribes which will make trouble for the Utes," said Sinawav. "But, the Utes, even though there aren't many, they are strong and brave."

Sinawav then scolded Coyote, "You are not responsible. From this time on you will wander the earth at night."

SOURCE: Adapted from: Wroth, William, (Ed.). Ute Indian Arts and Culture. Colorado Springs, CO: Colorado Springs Fine Art Center, 2000. Ute Creation Story told by Alden B. Naranjo and Monica Luhan. pp. 7-8

in Ignacio, Colorado. Another **band**, the Weeminuches, are the Ute Mountain Utes. Their headquarters are now in Towaoc, Colorado. The other four bands, Tabeguache (Uncompahgre), Yampa, White River, Grand River, are now called the Northern Utes. Today, the Northern Utes live on the Uintah-Ouray Reservation. Their headquarters are in Fort Duchesne, Utah.

When people move a lot and don't have **permanent** homes, they are called **nomads**. Nomads walk everywhere. They carry what they need on their backs. The Utes lived in small family groups most of the year. They were nomads and moved with the seasons. In the winter they lived on the plateaus and mesas where it is was warmer. In the spring, they moved to the mountains where it would be cooler in the summer.

Food was hard to find in the Great Basin. The Utes

kept moving to get the food that they needed. The people learned to take what they needed and nothing more. They protected the environment so they would have enough food for the next year.

When food is so hard to find, finding food was the most important job for the family. Everyone in the family worked to find food. When the mothers worked, the babies were safe in cradleboards. The cradleboards would lean against a tree. Sometimes their mothers carried them. There was very little time just for fun.

From the spring to the fall, the families would hunt for deer, elk, antelope, and other animals. Most of the game was found in the mountains. They would also gather pinon nuts, seeds, berries, roots, and other plants that they could eat. They would also eat snakes and insects if they were hungry!

With tools made of bone

Ute Cradleboard

and stone, they would plant corn, beans, and squash in the mountain meadows. They hoped it would stay warm enough to harvest these crops in the fall. Or, they might plant the crops before they went to the mountains. Then, they hoped that when they came back to the plateaus and canyons in the fall that there would be crops to harvest.

Navajo Cradleboard

Each family had a special place in the mountains. This place was where they knew they would find enough food to last them through the winter.

The old people learned about the weather, the trails, and where to find animals and plants for food. Then, they would teach the children. There were no books or writing, so the grandmothers and grandfathers told stories. The children listened to the stories and learned the important lessons. This is how they learned how to live in the Ute way.

When it got cold and snow began to fall in the mountains, Ute families would move from the mountains down into the mesas and plateaus. Now, the families could live close together in warm, protected places. If the winter was very cold and snowy, people stayed close to home to be warm and safe. Sometimes they didn't have enough food and they were hungry. Winter was a quiet time when they visited friends, played games, and told stories.

The Starving Time: A Story

There was no bright sun to greet this morning. The sky was heavy and gray. The howling wind blew all night long. It was a cold morning and it looked like snow was coming to their camp. Wolf, who was nine years old, wrapped a warm winter blanket around him. Grandmother had made his winter blanket. Carefully, she wrapped rabbit fur around strips of hide. Next, she wove the strips into a blanket. The blanket was soft and kept him warm on the coldest days and nights.

Their camp was nestled deep in a canyon. Wolf lived in a big wickiup with his Grandfather, Grandmother, Mother, Father, and baby sister, Little Deer. The high walls of the canyon protected their wickiup from the cold winds. The wickiup was covered with hides and soft grasses were on the floor. A stream was close by.

There were trees near the stream. It was Wolf's job to help find wood for the fire. The fire kept the family warm.

Yesterday, Wolf was playing a game with his sister and he forgot to bring enough wood for the fire. When night came, Grandfather told a story about the time Coyote foolishly forgot to get firewood. Wolf liked Grandfather's story. Today he will remember to bring in lots of wood for the fire.

Mother needed the fire to cook. The fire was burning brightly this morning. Wolf's stomach growled like a bear! He hoped that there would be something warm to eat. He liked corn mush, especially when it was cold outside. Maybe Mother would cook some mush for their morning meal.

They had a small crop of corn this year. His mother ground the corn with a mano and metate. In the fall, the women would gather together and grind corn and dried meat. Mother and Grandmother dried elk and deer meat on racks. Working with friends made the hard work easier. The berries that the women gathered were dried and mixed with fat. Then they were rolled into balls. The food was stored in a pit close to the wickiup.

Before the snow, Grandfather and Father climbed up the canyon to dig the big pit to store their food for winter. They lined the pit with rocks. All the food was put in large skin bags and placed in the pit. Wolf helped find more rocks to put on top of the pit. Then, Wolf helped the men build a big fire on top. Now, their pit was well hidden. If their food was taken by animals they would not have enough to eat in the winter. Wolf watched the men make the pit. He learned how to do the work that Ute men did.

Winter was a scary time in the Great Basin. Little animals were snug in their homes underground. Big game was hard to find. There were no growing plants. There were no berries or seeds to be found. If winter was very long with lots of snow, it would be hard to survive. Their family would be hungry. This is why winter was called the starving time. Wolf looked at the gray sky again. He didn't want any more snow to fall.

Mother fixed some corn mush for breakfast. But it was not a big breakfast. Wolf's stomach was still hungry. Only a little deer meat, a few vegetables, and some dried corn was left in the pit. They would have little to eat for dinner. They needed to find more food.

After everyone had eaten their mush, the family talked. Someone needed to go out to look for game. Grandmother and Mother started to mend the snowshoes. If the new snow was deep the snowshoes would made walking easier.

Little Deer was happy watching them work. She was wrapped in buckskin. Eagle down and deer hair kept her warm. Her cradle board was hung on a pole. Grandmother had made it to carry and protect her. It was decorated with fringe and painted yellow. If she had been a boy, it would have been painted white.

Grandfather made a plan. Wolf's grandparents were very wise and made many of the decisions for the family. Father and Mother would hunt for rabbits close to the stream. Rabbit stew would made a delicious meal. Father wanted to find an elk. If the snow was deep, it would be hard for elk to run. Grandfather had been sick, so he would stay home with Grandmother and take care of Wolf and Little Deer. While Mother and Father were looking for food, Grandfather would help Wolf gather firewood. Grandmother would weave berry baskets or maybe mend clothes for the Bear Dance in the spring.

If they can't find game, Mother and Father might bring back some tree bark. Bark could be eaten with salt or made into a broth. Wolf would rather eat rabbit stew. But bark would keep them alive.

Soon Mother and Father put on their winter clothes, warm moccasins with fur on the inside, and snowshoes. They went out to find food for the family. First, Father saw a rabbit in the brush by the stream. He asked the rabbit's permission to kill it for food. He thanked the rabbit for giving itself so they could eat. Later, he saw another rabbit. Again, he asked permission to take its life. They searched for elk for a long time, but no elk were seen. So, they decided to take some bark. They also asked a tree for its bark and thanked it for the gift. That is the way of the Ute. Mother knew the family would be happy tonight. On their way home, they thought of rabbit stew cooking by the fire.

Then Wolf saw his parents walking home. They were carrying some game. He began to think of stew too. Father cleaned the rabbits for eating. He saved the skin and fur for blankets and other things. Grandmother put special small rocks into the fire to get them very hot. She filled a large basket with water. When the rocks were hot, she dropped some of them into the basket. Slowly the water began to get hot too. In the pot went one rabbit. Next, a few roots and wild onions, and a little corn from the pit went in the pot. Tonight's meal would be hot and tasty. There would be enough stew for more meals. No one would go to sleep hungry. No one would be starving.

In the morning, Grandfather went to the door and raised his hands to the sun. The sun was bright. There was no more snow. He could smell spring in the air. The snow would start to melt today. Soon there would be plenty of food. Soon it would be time for the Bear Dance.

Wolf would dance in the Bear Dance for the first time. He would celebrate spring and the beginning of a new year. He thought about the hard winter and how the family worked together to survive. He would leave the worry about being hungry in the Bear Dance arena. He would begin the year with new thoughts of family, friends, and gathering food in the mountains for the next year.

There is no way to know the names of Ute people who lived so long ago. So the names in this story are not "real" names. They are just guesses about what people might have been called. In many Indian cultures, people are called by the name for their relationship to you. This is true today. So, in this story, Grandmother, Grandfather, Mother, and Father are used as the names for the adults.

When spring came, it was a time for celebrating a new year. When the last snow had fallen in the mountains, the Utes would celebrate the Bear Dance. The Utes tell a story about how the Bear Dance came to be.

How the Utes Learned the Bear Dance

The Utes have a story about how they first learned the Bear Dance. They said that a man went to sleep and had a dream about a bear. He dreamed that he should go to the mountains. A bear would teach him something of great strength. When he woke up, he went up to the mountain and saw a bear dancing back and forth. The bear spoke to the man who listened to his words of wisdom. Then the bear taught him how to do this dance and to sing the Bear Dance song. The man came home and  taught the dance and song to his people. For the Bear Dance, the Utes play and sing to the music of the morache or rasp. The music of the morache is supposed to sound like a bear waking from his long winter nap.

In the old times, the men prepared the Bear Dance corral for the dance and the feast. The women made the clothes that the their families wore to dance.

In the Bear Dance, the women ask the men to dance.

Northern Ute tribe Bear Dance photos © 2011 by Jennifer Orr

They walk to where the men are standing and flip the corner of their shawl in front of the man they chose. They dance to the music of the moraches. The **morache** is supposed to sound like a bear growling as he wakes up from his winter nap. The dance lasts a few days and ends with a feast. At the end of the dance, the dancers leave something special on a cedar tree in the corral. This is a **symbol** of leaving old troubles in the dance arena so the dancers can begin a new life and a new year!

Morache

The Bear Dance was just one of many dances. The Utes loved to sing and dance. Dances were a time to feast, visit, and play games with other families and neighbors. At the dances, people would also discuss family and tribal problems. Some dances were for fun and others were sacred or religious. The Sun Dance is a very important sacred dance.

The first thunder in the spring meant it was time to return to their summer homes. The people went back to the mountain valleys and parks. Spring and summer was a good time for the Utes. There was more food to eat and plenty of water.

The Utes had to move often. They needed homes that they could build quickly and easily. Their homes were called **wickiups**.

Wickiup

Wickiups were made of sticks and brush. It was easy to put up a new wickiup at each place that they camped. A brush home was often shaped like a tipi. First, a frame was made of poles. Then, brush and bark were put over the poles. Sometimes they put hides over the poles.

Wickiups were made in many sizes. When the Utes were in the mountains, the brush homes were small because they traveled so much to find food for the winter. When the Utes camped together in the winter, the wickiups were large enough to hold many people. They were sometimes as big as a tipi. The winter wickiups were made carefully. They needed to be strong in the winter.

A fireplace for cooking was in the middle of the wickiup. A fire also helped keep the people warm. Cooking was done outside as much as possible in the summer and winter. Wickiups were made on high places close to a spring or stream. It was good to have water close by. They were also built near trees. The trees could protect them in stormy weather and would give them wood for their fires.

Ute clothes were made of animal skins. They wore knee-high leggings made of soft animal skin tied with buckskin thongs. Their moccasins were made of rawhide. In the winter, they wore skins with the hair on the inside. It took about two or three deer skins to make a woman's dress. The women owned two dresses. They washed them in soap made from yucca roots. Ute men wore buck-skin aprons, leggings, and buckskin shirts. Clothes were decorated with fringe, animal claws, and elk teeth. Later, they decorated them with beads. When it was warm, the little children wouldn't wear any clothes!

The Ute made baskets to gather and store food. Berries and seeds were gathered in baskets. Some baskets were covered with pitch from pine trees so that they would hold water. Food was cooked by dropping hot stones into baskets of water. Or, they could roast food over the fire or in pits in the ground.

> **Tools**
>
> A Ute family would probably own:
> - ▣ a buckskin bag for clothing
> - ▣ a parfleche for meat
> - ▣ a berry basket
> - ▣ parching tray for toasting seeds
> - ▣ cups and spoons of wood and horn
> - ▣ some baskets or pots for boiling

The Utes traveled in family groups. Families made their own decisions and solved their own problems. They didn't need leaders. Everything changed when the Utes began to use horses in about 1630. Horses were brought to North America by the Spanish explorers. Horses made it possible to travel longer distances and they made hunting easier. Utes could then travel in large bands. Then the bands needed hunt leaders and war leaders for the tribe. Families still made their own decisions.

After the Plains Indians had horses, life became dangerous for the Utes. When the snow was gone from the mountain trails, the Plains Indians would come into Ute territory to hunt. The Utes had to protect their hunting grounds. But it worked the other way too! With horses, the Ute warriors could now travel to the Plains to hunt buffalo.

The Utes learned new ideas from the Plains Indians. They began to use tipis for their homes. Their chiefs began to wear Plains headdresses. They learned how to use a horse and **travois** to move their belongings. With horses, they had more food. The old ways began to change. Later, you will learn about the Ute traditions that are here today.

More Books to Read

Hobbs, Will. *Beardream*. New York, NY: Atheneum, 1997.

Raczek, Linda T. *The Night the Grandfathers Danced*. Flagstaff, AZ: Northland. 1995.

Videos to Watch

Anderson, P. (Producer). *Ute Legacy*. Ignacio, CO: Southern Ute Tribe/Colorado Historical Society, 1999. (available through the Southern Ute Museum)

Places to Go

The Ute Indian Museum & Ouray Memorial Park

Montrose, Colorado 81401
17253 Chipeta Drive
Phone: 970-249-3098

Southern Ute Museum and Cultural Center

Ignacio, Colorado

Music to Enjoy

Utes: Traditional Ute Songs (Vintage Collection, Vol. 10). Phoenix, AZ: Canyon Records 1998.

Websites to Visit

Ute Mountain Ute: http://www.utemountainute.com/

Southern Ute: http://www.southern-ute.nsn.us/

Southern Ute Museum: http://www.southernutemuseum.org

We Shall Remain a Native History of America and Utah:
http://www.kued.org/productions/weshallremain/ute/culture

Things to Do

Make a model of a wickiup

You will need to do some research about wikiups and then find the right materials in the environment.

Cooking with Rocks

Try to make a hard boiled egg by heating the water with hot rocks. You will need an adult to try this experiment.

Definitions

Band	a group of people who live and work together
Morache	a musical instrument made from a notched stick that rests on a drum; when it is rubbed, its sound is like the growl of a bear
Nomads	people who have no permanent home but move from place to place to gather food (plants, roots, berries) and hunt game (animals, birds, fish, insects)
Parfleche	a stiff box make of hide used like a suitcase to carry things
Permanent	stays the same or in the same place
Symbol	something that stands for something else
Travois	two poles attached on each side of a dog or horse with the ends dragging on the dirt behind the animal; supplies and belongings were fastened to the poles so that the animals could travel with larger loads.
Wickiup	temporary camp shelters that were used before and shortly after the Ute obtained the horse.

Dancing Teepees

High up in the Rocky Mountains
Dancing teepees
Dance on the grassy banks of
Cripple Creek
With laughing fringes in the
autumn sun.

Indian children
Play with bows and arrows
On the grassy banks of Cripple
Creek.

Indian women
Gather kindling
To start an evening fire.

Dancing Teepees

Dance against the fire-lighted
autumn trees.

Braves returning
Home from raiding
Gallantly ride into camp
With horses, scalps, and ornaments.

Dancing teepees
Sleep now on the grassy banks of
Cripple Creek
High up in the Rocky Mountains.

Calvin O'John, Ute-Navajo

SOURCE: Sneve, V. D. H. Dancing Teepees. New York, NY: Holiday House, 1989. pp. 20-21.

Chapter 5

Cheyenne and Arapaho Life in the Past

Beaded bandolier bag

Grace's school has an Indian Club that meets after school. She really likes to go to Indian Club. The Indian kids come to learn about their Indian cultures and history. They learn how Indian people contributed to American life. They also learn traditional crafts like beading. Her Indian friends like to be together.

The kids that go to Indian club belong to many different tribes. Some have lived in Denver all of their lives. Others moved to Denver from other towns, cities, or their reservations.

Elders from different tribes come to Indian Club to tell traditional stories. They also tell about the times when they were children and about their tribal history and leaders. Other Indian people come to share some of their traditional skills. Grace's grandmother visited the club to tell about traditional Cheyenne weddings and the women's Quilling **Society**.

At Indian Club, Grace learns about American and Cheyenne history. She wants to know about the Cheyenne lifeways of long ago. She knows that the Cheyenne and Arapaho were friends in the past. They were alike in many ways and different in many ways too. She is interested in learning about how Cheyenne and Arapaho men provided for and protected their families. She wants to learn how the women took care of their homes and families. How did children play? Did they go to school?

Along with Grace and her friends, let's step backwards in time and learn how the Cheyenne and Arapaho lived on the Plains before Colorado was a state. Knowing Indian history is part of understanding American history—if you are Indian or not!

In the 1600s, the Cheyennes probably lived in what is now Minnesota. Then they moved west and settled in North Dakota and South Dakota. The arrival of the Europeans had forced them from the woodlands. They lived in earth homes and grew corn. Their culture changed when they got horses. They "gave up the corn." That means that they stopped growing corn and began hunting buffalo on the Plains. Soon they were very skilled with raising and riding horses. They became good hunters and strong warriors. In the past, the Cheyenne called themselves, Tsis-tsis'-tas, or "The People." They still use this traditional name.

Two Nations

1803 - Arapaho and Cheyenne tribes separated. Northern Cheyenne and Arapaho moved north of the South Platte River, Southern Cheyenne and Arapaho lived along the Arkansas River.

The Arapaho called themselves Inuna-ina or "Our People." The roots of the Arapaho people are also in the woodlands of the Northeast Culture Area. They were hunters and gatherers. Later, they probably were farmers too. Like the Cheyenne, they moved (or were pushed) west onto the Great Plains. In the early 1800s, fur trappers met Arapahos in Colorado.

After they moved onto the Plains, the Cheyenne and Arapaho quickly became friends. They also had the same enemies, the Crow, Shoshone, Pawnee, Kiowa, Apache, Sioux, and Ute. People became enemies when they wanted the same hunting grounds or needed more horses. The Arapahos believed that the Man-Above created the Rocky Mountains to keep them safe from the Utes and Shoshones.

These tribes spoke different Algonquian languages that were spoken by tribes in the woodlands in the East. This is one way that we know that the Cheyenne and Arapaho once lived in that part of the country. The Cheyenne and Arapaho still had to use some sign language to understand each other.

The people of both tribes loved and honored their children. New babies were gifts to their families and tribes. Children were never hit or punished. Grandparents, aunts, and uncles all helped take care of them. Children were taught how the people of their tribes acted and what they believed. Grandparents would tell stories to teach the children what was right and what was wrong. Stories also taught them about their tribal history and beliefs.

The children did not go to school like children do today. They learned what they needed to know from stories and from playing, watching, and helping. Boys were taught how to do the work that the men did. Girls learned how to do women's work. Men took care of their families by protecting them and hunting food. Women cooked and prepared the food, made clothing, and took care of the home and children. The work of men and women was very important. Everyone worked together for their families and the tribe.

Girls played with toy tipis and made cradleboards for their dolls. They watched their mother work and helped to get firewood

Storytelling

"An old storyteller would smooth the ground in front of him with his hand and make two marks in it with his right thumb, two with his left, and a double mark with both thumbs together. Then he touched the marks on the ground with both hands and rubbed them together and passed them over his head and all over his body. That meant the Creator had made human beings' bodies and their limbs as he had made the earth, and that the Creator was witness to what was to be told."

SOURCE: Stands in Timber, John and Margot Liberty. Cheyenne Memories. Lincoln, NE: University of Nebraska, 1972. p. 12.

and water. Later, they learned to sew and dress buffalo hides. They would help gather plants and berries. Their grandmothers often taught them to cook.

Boys were given bows and arrows and learned to shoot small animals. They had games and races that helped them become strong and good hunters. They learned to ride horses and make weapons. They also helped in the buffalo hunts by bringing water or keeping the fire.

Horses were very important to both tribes. First, a baby would ride on a horse with its mother. Or, the baby might ride in a cradle-board beside its mother or on a **travois** behind a horse. By the time the children were about five years old, they were taught to ride gentle horses. The boys also learned how to care for the horses and were responsible for taking them to graze and drink water.

In many ways the Cheyenne and Arapaho were alike because they had the same environment and natural resources on the Great Plains. But they were different in other ways. They had different leaders and ways to live together peacefully. They also had different sacred beliefs, ceremonies, and celebrations. First, let's explore how the people of these two tribes used the resources in the same environment. Then, we will explore how the Cheyenne and Arapaho developed different ways of making decisions in their communities. They also had sacred ceremonies and celebrations that were different.

The buffalo was really the hardware store, the drugstore, the toy store, the clothing store, and the supermarket for Plains Indian people. How many ways do you think the buffalo was used? Look at this list! WOW!

Uses of the Buffalo

Hides

Tipi covers
Bedding
Clothing
Shields
Sheaths
Saddles
Bags and pouches
Ropes, tie strings
Water troughs
Horseshoes
Toboggans
Masks
Headdresses
Balls
Dolls

Sinew
(tissue joining muscle and bone)

Thread
Bow strings

Droppings
(buffalo chips)

Fuel
Diapers (chips were ground)

Bones

Scraping tools
Paint brushes
Sled runners
Dice

Organs

Buckets, basins
Glue
Hide softener

Fat

Hide softener
Pipe polish

Hair

Ornaments
Stuffing

Horns

Arrow points
Masks
Headdress ornaments
Powder flasks
Spoons
Cups

Hooves

Glue
Rattles

Tails

Ornaments
Fly Swatters

Buffalo (or Bison) are huge animals and very fast and strong . They are over 12 feet long and about 6 1/2 feet tall. Their tails are about 3 feet long. They weigh from 1,200 to 2,000 pounds. They can run about 35 miles an hour and swim rivers over 1/2 mile wide. When they bellow, they can be heard for up to 3 miles.

The Cheyenne and Arapaho had many ways to hunt. Before they had horses to help them, they had to hunt on foot. One way was to sneak up on the buffalo. Sometimes a hunter would cover himself with the skin of a wolf. The buffalo herd would not be afraid of just one wolf, so a hunter could get close enough to shoot with his bow and arrow.

Sometimes in the heavy snow of winter they would use snow shoes to track the buffalo. The buffalo couldn't run very fast in the snow and they could be easily killed. Sometimes many people would surround the animals with fire or stone walls and force them to run into a small area where they could be trapped and killed. Also, they would drive them off cliffs. Many buffalo were killed when they fell. Some people say that a man could live for 200 days on the meat of one buffalo!

Horses changed how people hunted. The Indians of the Plains trained their horses so that they could ride close to the running buffalo. The Indian riders used their legs to guide the horse. Then they could use both hands to shoot arrows. They learned to ride on the side of their horses for protection when they hunted or were in battle. Good horses were needed to hunt buffalo!

Not only could horses carry hunters a long way to find food, they could carry people and their belongings on travois. A travois was made of two poles tied together at the top. It looked a little like an "A". Strips of rawhide went from side to side of the travois.

Clothes, cooking pots, blankets, and even babies and old people were put on the travois. The travois was attached to dogs or horses who dragged the travois behind them like a sled. The travois

helped people move their things from one camp to another. It was also used to carry meat, hides, and firewood to the camp. With horses, the people could move faster, easier, and carry more things.

Horses were important in war too. A warrior depended on his horse. One way Indian warriors brought honor to themselves was by counting

Crow Warrior. From a drawing by Dario Weilec. Used with permission of the artist.

coup. Counting coup was very brave. A warrior would ride close to an enemy. Then, instead of killing him, he would just touch him with a long stick. This showed how brave he was.

Horses were also a reason people went to war. They were so valuable that warriors would ride out to take horses from another camp. Taking horses from another tribe was not a crime. It was a way of counting coup.

If a man owned many horses, he was rich. He would give horses to families that had lost their horses. Or he might share his horses when it was time to move camp or go on a hunt. Because he was so **generous**, he was admired by the people. A young man had to have many horses before he could get married. He would give horses to the family of the woman he wanted to marry.

**Eagle Claw
Coup Stick**

When the Cheyenne and Arapaho moved to the Plains, they began to use tipis. Because horses could carry heavy loads, the people could make larger, more comfortable tipis. Tipis were warm and cozy in winter and breezy and cool in summer. A tipi starts with three poles tied together at the top. Then other long poles are added. The tipi is covered with buffalo skins.

Women were in charge of making and taking care of the tipis. To make a tipi, they spread fresh buffalo hides on the ground. Then they used scrapers to take off the flesh and the hair. The hides were soaked in water for a few days. Then they were rubbed with buffalo fat, liver, and brains. This rubbing made the hides soft. The hides were rinsed in water many times. The last step was to rub them over a rawhide thong. This made the hides even softer. Many tribes smoked the hides to give them a beautiful color.

Now the hides were ready to cut to the right shape. The women cut and sewed about 15 buffalo hides to cover the tipi. The cover was put on a pole and raised to the top of the tipi frame. Then, the women wrapped it around the frame. A hole was on top for the smoke. Flaps at the top kept the rain out. Women were in charge of the tipis. After a hard day of traveling, two women could put up a tipi in about fifteen minutes.

The doorway of the tipi faced east to greet the first rays of the morning sun. A hide covered the door. Many of the tipis were decorated with pictures of battles and dreams. The Cheyenne rubbed their tipis with white clay to make them white. People could tell if a tipi was a Cheyenne tipi!

To keep tipis warm in the winter, the people would build walls of earth or brush around the tipi. They also had a dew cloth on the inside of the tipi that would hang from the walls on the inside. The dew cloth went from about shoulder height to the ground. It would keep the tipi dry and warm. In the summer, the bottom of the tipi could be lifted in places to make it cooler.

SOURCE: Yue, D. & Yue. C. The tipi. New York, NY: Alfred A. Knopf, 1984. p. 54.

Many people lived close together in the camp. It was important to respect everyone's feelings and privacy. If the door of the tipi was open, everyone could come in. If it was closed, people would cough or call out and then wait to be invited inside.

Men sat on the right side of the tipi and women sat on the south side. It was not polite to walk between a person and the fire.

Gatherings in the tipi would usually begin with a prayer. The host would offer people food. Leftovers were taken home by the guests. Tipis were the place for good conversations, stories, and jokes. Some tipis were used as sacred places.

A New Cheyenne Family: A Story

There was something special in the air. Little Hawk could feel and almost smell the excitement. Mother and Grandmother were busy doing their chores like they did every morning. But today something was different. Everyone seemed busier than usual, everyone was happier than usual, and even the food starting to cook in the fire was beginning to smell tastier than ever! Little Hawk had already made two trips to get fresh water and firewood for the fire!

No one said that was going to be a special day. But Little Hawk noticed that father was spending more time grooming the horses. Some of his relatives came for short visits. His Aunt had gone out early to search for wild onions for the cooking pot. Magpie, his sister, was smiling, her hair was shining, and she was singing softly as she worked. He just knew that something good was going to happen today!

Little Hawk walked out to his favorite place near the stream to sit on his special rock. He needed to do some thinking. What else was different in the camp? What was going on? All of a sudden he had an idea. It was a good idea, too.

Well, he knew that Red Elk, a tall, handsome young man in the camp, had spent much time with the raiding parties in the last few years and was building his herd of horses. He had been brave in battle and had counted coup. He had shared his first buffalo kill with an old man. He was becoming known as a generous man. People respected his generosity and bravery.

Last spring, Little Hawk noticed that when Magpie went to get water or wood, Red Elk was close by. If he tried to talk to her, she would would stop to talk for a few minutes. She didn't keep on walking, which was a sign that she wasn't interested in him at all.

Then Red Elk started to come to their tipi with a blanket. He waited for Magpie to come outside. Then he would throw the blanket around her and they would talk under the blanket. This happened so often that Little Hawk didn't even think much about it. He had other things to do and games to play with his friends. But, now he knew what was going to happen. If he was right, there would be a wedding soon! A wedding was really special.

Cheyenne women were treated with much respect. When a man found a woman that he wanted to marry, he asked an older relative, usually a woman, to visit the home of the woman he wanted to be his wife. This woman brought gifts to the bride and talked about the man who wanted to marry her. She would tell about his bravery, kindness, and courage. After the visitor left, the family would talk about the proposal. The next day, they would announce if the couple would marry. The woman could decide not to marry the man, but she usually agreed.

Little Hawk knew what was going to happen, even if no one was talking about it. He thought that Red Elk was ready to have a bride. He also thought his sister wanted Red Elk to be her husband.

It wasn't long before Father stepped inside the tipi to announce that they had a visitor. An old woman stood quietly inside the tipi until everyone was quiet. Then she said, "Red Elk wishes to marry Magpie. He has sent many horses and gifts to show his respect for her and family." Then she turned and left.

Mother told Little Hawk to run to the lodges of his relatives and tell them to come quickly to their tipi. The family would discuss Red Elk's proposal. Would he be a good husband to Magpie? Did she want to be his wife? They knew that Red Elk was strong, brave and good. Magpie's soft smile told them that she wanted to be his wife.

It wasn't long before the decision was made. The family went outside and unpacked the many gifts that were loaded on the horses. They divided up all of Red Elk's gifts. Then they went to their own homes with the gifts. Little Hawk's tipi became very quiet. It was time to sleep. There would be much excitement tomorrow.

In the morning the family gathered again. This time they brought their own belongings and gifts to give to Red Elk's family. They brought tools, arrows, shields, and many horses. They brought more horses to give away than Red Elk had given them. Magpie's father gave his best horse.

Magpie dressed in her most beautiful buckskin dress. It was decorated with quills and feathers. The women brushed her hair and painted her face. She was so beautiful. When they were ready to ride to Red Elk's tipi, the men put her on a fine horse. An old woman, who was not one of their relatives, led Magpie's horse to Red Elk's lodge. Magpie's mother and the other women relatives followed her with the other horses. All of their relatives followed. What a happy parade!

When they arrived at Red Elk's lodge, his family gently took Magpie off of her horse and set her on a special blanket. Red Elk's four brothers picked up the blanket and carried Magpie into the tipi. His relatives dressed her in their finest robe and gave her beautiful gifts.

Then the families had a fine feast. It was a feast of happiness, sharing, and celebrating a new family. The next day, Magpie and Red Elk returned to Magpie's family. They were now a married couple.

Little Hawk knew why everyone in his family had been so busy. His mother, grandmothers, and aunts had prepared many buffalo hides for a new tipi. Now, the women of the camp would help them sew them together and put up a tipi for the new family. It was a Cheyenne custom for new families to live close to the bride's family. Magpie's mother and Red Elk's mother would give them pots, dishes, and beds.

Little Hawk was happy to see the new tipi and the smiles of Magpie and Red Elk. There was now a new Cheyenne family in the camp.

Arapaho Marriage

An Arapaho wedding was much like a Cheyenne wedding. When a man wanted to marry a woman, he brought horses to her family. If they accepted, the woman's family gave gifts to the man's family. The families set up a tipi. The leaders prayed and gave them advice for a happy marriage. A feast was held and more gifts were given. Then the man and the woman were married. This is one reason, young men needed to have lots of horses.

Cheyenne Leaders

When families began to live in communities, they chose leaders and found fair ways to solve problems and make decisions for the communities.

The Cheyenne had ten bands. A band was a group of families. A man could become a chief of his band if he was a skilled warrior and was respected by friends and enemies. Chiefs were responsible for peace in the tribe and with other tribes. They had to be strong warriors and able to keep peace for their people. They had to be calm, wise, generous, kind, and courageous. They took care of the poor and those who needed help.

Four chiefs from each of the ten Cheyenne bands and the four men who were the principal chiefs, were called the Council of Forty-Four. This council made decisions that affected the whole tribe. The council members were peace chiefs.

The war chiefs were the leaders of the five military societies for Cheyenne men. They were the Fox, Elk, Shield, Dog, and Bowstring societies. They had dances and songs that could only be done by society members. Each society also had its own ceremonies, sacred objects, and special clothes. The Dog Soldier society became famous because it fought long and hard against the United States Army. The men in the societies were warriors. Like today's police, they also kept peace in the bands and made sure

Cheyenne Military Societies

- ■ Fox
- ■ Elk
- ■ Shield
- ■ Bowstring
- ■ Dog

Quilled war shirt

Quilled eagle wing fan

that the people followed the rules of the camp.

Cheyenne women had their own societies. They were as important as the men's societies. The best known was the Quilling Society. The members made beautifully quilled buffalo robes and other items for honored members of the tribe. The societies honored the women who made such beautiful things.

The Arapaho did not have a principal chief. Each band had its own leaders. They usually had a peace chief and a war chief. The peace chief was responsible for everyday activities. He settled problems between people. He would decide when to move the camp. The war chief took over when the tribe went on raids. The chiefs of the bands formed a council for the whole tribe. They made decisions for the tribe.

The military societies or **lodges** of the Arapaho had grades. This means that they moved up to a new society as they got older. Men who did not join the lodges could never earn responsible positions or respect in the community.

Boys about 12 years old first joined the Kit Fox society. Boys would ask a older man to be their adviser. He taught them the songs and dances of the ceremonies. The boys promised to help each other for the rest of their lives. After they proved their skill and bravery, they became Star Men in the Star Ceremony.

Arapaho Military Societies

- Kit Fox (about 12 years old)
- Star Lodge (about 15-16 years old)
- Tomahawk Lodge (about 17-25 years old)
- Spear Lodge (about 20-35 years old)
- Crazy Lodge (about 30-45 years old)
- Dog Lodge (about 45-55 years old)
- Stoic Lodge (older men)
- Offerings Lodge (all ages)
- Water-Pouring-Old-Men (Seven old men who directed all the lodge ceremonies)

As they got older, men joined the next society. Each society had its own songs, dances, dress, and medicine bundles. The Tomahawk Lodge was the first lodge. The Spear Lodge was next. The Crazy Lodge was the third lodge. At about age 50, men could join the Dog Lodge. Dog Men directed battles and became tribal leaders. The Stoic Lodge ceremony was for men about 60 years old.

The most respected men were called the "Water-Pouring Old Men." These seven men cared for the sacred flat pipe. When the bands camped together in the summer, these men prayed every day in a large "sweat lodge" in the center of the camp. These ceremonies protected and guided the Arapahos on their path through life.

Arapaho women belonged to the Buffalo Lodge. The most respected women were called the Seven Old Women. Their medicine bags held the materials needed to teach the skills of making and decorating tipis, clothes, bags, and other tribal materials. The decorations were very important to the people.

The Cheyenne had two important sacred objects. These objects were the Four Sacred Arrows and the Buffalo Hat. There were four arrows in a sacred bundle. Two arrows were for hunting so the people would not be hungry. Two arrows were for warfare so the Cheyenne would be safe.

The Buffalo Hat or Sacred Medicine Hat was kept in a bag of buffalo hide. Two painted horns are on the hat and it is covered with blue beads. It was shown when many of the tribe were sick, when the Sacred Arrows were renewed, and sometimes when in battle. The Sacred Arrows and the Buffalo Hat are kept in special tipis where keepers take care of them.

The people believed that if they had respect for these objects, they would have good health and long lives. The objects would help them hunt and have victory over their enemies. They are still honored in the same way by the Cheyenne today.

There were many sacred ceremonies in Cheyenne life. The most important ceremony was the Renewal of the Sacred Arrows. This ceremony was brought to them by Sweet Medicine, a man who came to the people when they lived near the Black Hills. On longest day of year, the ten bands of the Cheyenne put their tipis in a circle. Inside the circle is the lodge of the Keeper of the Arrows. A medicine man led special **rituals** for four days. The medicine man replaced the **sinew** and feathers on the four sacred arrows. Only the men could look at the arrows. At the end of the

Cheyenne & Arapaho Sundance lodge—ca. 1898

four days, they all cleaned themselves before going back to regular life.

The Sun Dance is also an important ceremony. It was held once a year to honor the strength of the sun and to pray for the earth. The Sun Dance was held in the summer. These ceremonies are still held by today's traditional Cheyennes.

A very important object used in Arapaho ceremonies was the Flat Pipe. It was important in the Arapaho creation story. Arapaho people believe that this story is sacred and shouldn't be shared with other people. The Flat Pipe is still sacred to the Arapaho people.

Cheyenne & Arapaho Sundance lodge interior—ca. 1898

The Arapaho people believe in a Great Spirit called Man-Above. Many of their ceremonies were about the sun that gives life.

The Offerings Lodge or Sun Dance was held every summer. The dancers would pray for nature and for the tribe. They danced in a circle with a sacred tree trunk in the center. A rawhide doll was usually tied to the top of the sacred tree. The dancers danced for days without food or water. The Sun Dance is still held today.

The Arapaho Four Hills of Life

Hill	Age	Four Directions	Four Seasons
First Hill	Childhood	East	Spring
Second Hill	Youth	South	Summer
Third Hill	Adulthood	West	Fall
Fourth Hill	Old Age	North	Winter

After death, a person could be born again.

More Books to Read:

Bial, Raymond. *The Cheyenne*. New York, NY: Benchmark 2001.

Bial, Raymond. *The Arapaho*. New York, NY: Benchmark, 2004.

Clark, Ann Nolan. *There Are Still Buffalo* (reprint). Santa Fe, NM: Ancient City, 1992.

Gibson, Karen B. *The Arapaho: Hunters of the Plains*. Mankato, MN: Bridgestone, 2003.

Goble, Paul. *Remaking the Earth: A Creation Story From the Great Plains of North America*. New York, NY: Orchard, 1996.

Goble, Paul. *Storm Maker's Tipi*. New York, NY: Atheneum, 2001.

Korman, Susan. *Horse Raid: An Arapaho Camp in the 1800s*. Norwalk, CT: Soundprints and the Smithsonian Institution, 1998.

Roop, Peter. *The Buffalo Jump*. Flagstaff, AZ: Northland, 1996.

Sneve, Virginia. *Driving Hawk*. The Cheyennes. New York, NY: Holiday House, 1996.

Terry, Michael. *Bad Hand*. Daily Life in a Plains Indian Village 1868. New York, NY: Clarion, 1999.

Yue, David & Charlotte Yue. *The Tipi*. New York, NY: Alfred A. Knopf, 1984.

Places to Go:

Colorado History Museum
1300 Broadway
Denver, CO 80203
Phone: 303-866-3682

Music to Enjoy:

Northern Cheyenne Sun Dance Songs.
Indian House, NM. http://www.indianhouse.com

Arapaho music
http://www.colorado.edu/csilw/arapahoproject/music/index.html

Websites to Visit:

Colorado Historical Society http://www.coloradohistory.org

Northern Cheyenne Nation http://www.cheyennenation.com

Things to Do

Make a Parfleche

Plains Indians made large hide envelopes to store and carry food and clothing. They could hang a parfleche from tipi poles, a saddle, and a travois.

What You Need:
- ◼ A large brown paper bag
- ◼ 4 pieces of yarn, 8 inches long
- ◼ Crayons or markers
- ◼ Hole punch

What To Do:
1. Cut the paper bag into a rectangle. Make any size you like.
2. Fold it in thirds lengthwise and crosswise. Open it up.
3. Trim off the corners and ends.
4. Decorate with crayons or markers. Use triangles, diamonds, and lines.
5. Fold it along the creases.
6. Punch 2 holes on each end, thread yarn through the holes and tie it closed.

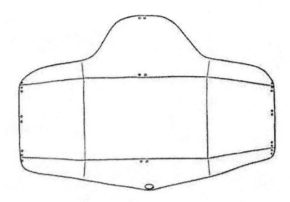

SOURCE: Carlson, Laurie. 1994. *More Than Moccasins*. Chicago, IL: Chicago Review Press. p. 24.

Tell a Story on a Buffalo Hide

The Indians of the Plains remembered things that happened by drawing pictures on a buffalo hide. This was one way to remember important events. These stories on buffalo hides were their history books. What story do you think is being told on the buffalo skin pictured below?

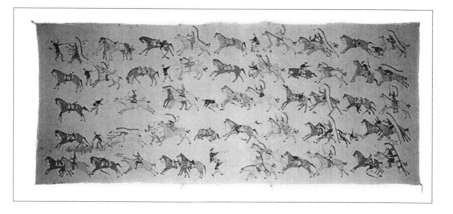

What You Need:

A large brown grocery sack, and crayons (use earth tones, browns, yellows, oranges, grays, and black).

What To Do:

1. Cut the seams of a big brown grocery sack. Lay it out flat. Dip the bag quite quickly in a basin of water. Taking it out carefully, scrunch it up several times. Now, smooth it out flat again and let it dry. Do this several times, if possible.

2. Use a pencil to lightly draw the shape of a buffalo hide. When you have a shape you like, cut out your buffalo hide.

3. On a piece of paper, plan the drawing for your buffalo hide. Your story can be about your neighborhood, a sport you play, your school or classroom, your friends, your family, a pet, or a special occasion in your life.

4. Draw the story on your buffalo hide with crayons.

5. Ask a friend to "read" your story.

SOURCE: Hoig, Stan. (1989). The Cheyenne. New York, NY: Chelsea. (center section.)

Make Meatless Pemmican

In traditional times, Plains Indians made pemmican from dried buffalo meat combined with nuts, dried berries. Now pemmican can be made without meat if you don't have buffalo. This recipe makes 12 servings.

What You Need:
- 1/2 cup cornmeal
- 1/2 cup raisins
- 1/2 cup peanuts
- 1/2 cup hickory or other kind of nut pieces
- 1/2 cup dried apples
- 1/2 cup honey or maple syrup

What To Do:
1. Spread cornmeal in a thin layer on a cookie sheet and place it in a warm oven (set at lowest possible setting) for 15 to 30 minutes. Check it frequently to make sure it doesn't burn. Take it out when it is completely dry.
2. Chop the raisins, nuts, and apples into very small pieces.
3. Combine the nuts, raisins, apples, and cornmeal.
4. Add the honey or maple syrup to the dry ingredients. Blend together.
5. Divide the mixture into 1/2 cup portions and press them into small cakes.

The cakes can be stored in the refrigerator and eaten when desired.

SOURCE: Bonvillain, N. *The Cheyennes: People of the Plains.* Brookfield, CT: Millbrook, (1996). p. 28

Definitions

Generous	to give away much
Lodge	a lodge can be a home, or it can mean a club of members who share beliefs and ceremonies that are alike.
Parfleche	an untanned animal skin folded to make a carrying case
Ritual	a special way of doing things
Sinew	an animal tendon that is used as a cord or thread
Society	a military society is like a club
Travois	a type of sled used by Indian peoples to carry goods, made of two joined poles dragged by a horse or dog.

Chapter 6

Terrible Times and Change for the Cheyenne and Arapaho

It was a warm summer evening and the sun was going down. Grace and her grandmother had just finished weeding the flowers in the garden. They worked hard and now they were ready for a rest and a glass of Grandmother's lemonade. This was a good evening for a story! Grace leaned close to her grandmother. She asked her to tell the stories about life for the Cheyenne people after the miners, farmers, and settlers came to Colorado. How did their lives change when the Americans came?

Her grandmother looked down and was quiet for a long time. Slowly, she said she that needed to think about Grace's questions. The stories about this time were passed from one generation to the next. Her grandparents had told the stories to her. These were the stories of the Cheyenne people who lived during the 1800s. That was more than 200 years ago. They were stories of fear and sadness. It was very hard for her to think about this terrible time. It would be hard to tell the stories to Grace.

The stories about this sad time long ago are painful for Indian people to remember. All Indians except the Utes were moved from Colorado by force. Treaties were made and broken. Terrible battles were fought. Indian people lost their homelands and their ways of taking care of their families. Many Indians died from new diseases, **starved**, or were killed in battles. The Americans wanted them to change their beliefs, values, and ways of taking care of their families. They wanted them to speak only English and forget their languages. It was a time of great danger and change for the Cheyenne, Arapaho, Utes, and all of the Indian people living, hunting, and trading in Colorado.

When the Americans came to Colorado, they wrote stories about their life here. They wrote letters, diaries, and newspapers. Sometimes these written stores were correct and sometimes they were not. Sometimes they made wrong actions seem like right actions. Sometimes the whole story wasn't told. People didn't have television or radio or video cameras to really see what really happened so long ago. So most people in America believed the stories they read.

Some Important Leaders in the Terrible Times

- Black Kettle (Southern Cheyenne) c.1803-1868
- George Bent (Southern Cheyenne-American) 1843-1918
- Niwot or Left Hand (Southern Arapaho) c. 1820s -1864
- Little Raven (Southern Arapaho). c. 1820 -1889)
- Silas Soule (Commander of Calvary Company D, 1st Colorado Cavalry) 1838-1865
- White Antelope (Southern Cheyenne) 1796-1864

The stories of the Indians were not written. They were told. Indian people even memorized the stories so the next generation would know what happened long ago. Often they drew pictures in **ledgerbooks** or on animal skins to help them remember important things that happened.

For a long time, people knew only the stories written by the white people. Now we know that the stories that Indian people told, painted, and even sung were important too. They told another part of the story. The Indian side about what happened when the American people came to settle in Colorado is very important to understand, even if it is hard to talk about.

Grace's grandmother thought about telling her granddaughter about this time of danger and change. Not only were the stories very hard to tell, they were also hard to understand. Some were about cruel actions, dishonest people, and broken promises. There were good people and bad people. What was the right way to tell these stories? She decided to tell Grace about this time of hardship and sadness with honesty. She wanted Grace to learn about the history of her people and how they were almost destroyed. But also, she wanted to tell her about the courage and bravery of Indian leaders and how Indian people and their cultures survived and continue today.

Good things can come from sad stories. These stories, like many Indian stories, are stories that teach. There are lessons in them. Maybe if people learn these lessons the bad things that happened so long ago won't happen again.

Wiping away a few soft tears, Grace's grandmother smiled. Now she was ready to sit beside Grace and tell her the stories of danger and change in the lives of Indian people in Colorado.

Grace's Grandmother Tells A Story

The story begins with the land. It was hard to grow crops on the dry plains, on the high plateaus, and in the mountains. The Utes, Cheyenne, Arapaho, and others had to roam far to hunt buffalo. They needed plenty of land to gather their food. The people who came to Colorado wanted the lands of the Indians to hunt buffalo and other animals, to raise crops and animals, to mine for gold and silver, and to build trails, railroads, and towns.

What happened when the needs of the settlers and the needs of the Indians were different? Listen carefully to these stories and remember the land and the lifeways of the Indian people.

Long ago, before Colorado was a state, there was a time when the Indians and the Americans who lived in Colorado lived in peace. The 1830s were a time of trading. Trading was good for

Bent's Old Fort, from a drawing made by a U.S. Cavalry officer.

everyone. It was a time of well being. Trading was sharing and people were learning from each other.

Many things were happening at about the same time. I will try to explain only a few of the most important events that brought terrible change for the Cheyenne and Arapaho people. There is much to tell and much to learn.

For the Cheyenne, Arapaho, Kiowa, Comanche, and other Plains Indians, the Santa Fe Trail that opened in 1821 was very important. Bent's Fort was built in 1833 along the Santa Fe Trail by William Bent, his brother Charles, and partner, Ceran St. Vrain. The fort was built above the Arkansas River, on a bluff close to today's town of La Junta. The fort was close to the mountain men

A reconstruction of Bent's Old Fort. You can see the buffalo robe press in the foreground on the right.

who trapped beaver and other animals. It was also near the hunting grounds of the Plains Indians.

It wasn't long before the beaver were almost gone and their skins weren't in style any more. Now, the Americans in the East wanted the warm, heavy buffalo hides or robes from the Plains. The buffalo robes were used as blankets or made into coats, saddles, or belts. There was a large buffalo robe press in the plaza or center area of the Bent's Fort. The press would pack ten buffalo robes into a huge **bale** or package that made it easier to send them to people in the East. In 1840, about 15,000 buffalo robes were sent East!

The Indians of the Plains traded the buffalo hides or robes for things that would make their lives easier. They traded for iron kettles for cooking, beads for decorating clothes and moccasins, cotton and heavy canvas for clothes and tipis, and mirrors and metal for starting fires. They also wanted knives, tobacco, guns, and blankets.

The Cheyenne, Arapaho, Sioux, Comanche, Kiowa and Apache people came to trade at Bent's Fort. Often villages of Cheyenne and Arapaho camped just outside the walls of the fort. People said that four languages were spoken at Bent's Fort, English, Spanish, French, and Indian.

The fort was built like a town with walls all around it. Inside the fort there were blacksmith, gunsmith, carpenter, and barber shops. There also were a kitchen and dining room, trade and meeting rooms, sleeping rooms for the workers, nicer rooms for very important people, and storehouses. Two large towers protected the people. The horses and mules were kept in a corral with cactus planted on top of the wall to keep them safe.

Traders, soldiers, and visitors who came to the fort were served tasty food on plates with knives and forks. Visitors and traders on their way to Santa Fe could play games like billiards, chess, or backgammon or race their horses. Dances were held for the visitors and people who lived at the fort.

Later, William Bent decided to build a new fort in another place. He wanted to sell his first fort to the government. But, the government didn't buy the fort and it soon burned to the ground. Many people thought that William Bent set the fire. Soon, he built another fort thirty-five miles away which was called Big Timbers. Later this fort was called Fort Wise.

In 1840 the Plains Indians of Colorado came together to make peace with their enemies. So many people were killed when Indians fought each other, that the tribes decided that they wanted peace. The Cheyenne Dog Soldiers planned a peace meeting. Thousands of Indians came together and made camp along the Arkansas River, close to Bent's Fort.

The Cheyenne, Arapaho, Kiowa, Comanche, and Apache warriors decided that they would not fight each other. They would fight together against their enemies. For days they exchanged gifts

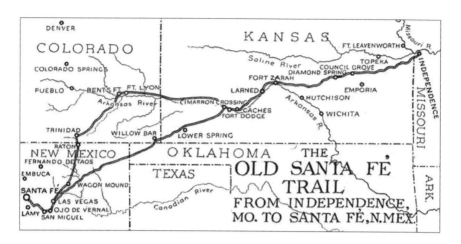

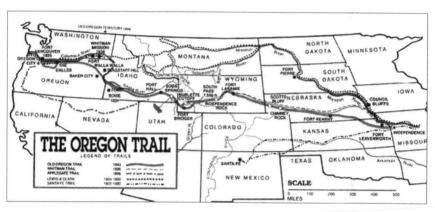

to celebrate the peace. The Kiowa and Comanche gave away thousands of horses. Everyone received at least one horse and sometimes more. A great feast was held. This peace was never broken. Because trade was so important to the Indians, these tribes stayed friendly with the traders too.

The Santa Fe Trail began in Kansas and wound its way through Colorado on the way to New Mexico. It was used by traders, travelers, and soldiers. The Oregon Trail went along just north of Colorado. Long wagon trains of miners on their way to the gold fields in California traveled along the Oregon Trail. The miners hoped to get rich and the settlers or **pioneers** wanted to start new lives

Something to Think About: The Oregon Trail

The people who rode in wagons along the Oregon Trail were families who wanted a better life in the West. They walked about 2000 miles across the plains and the mountains. They thought the land was free and didn't belong to anyone. But the land was home to many Indian tribes. The land provided everything that their families needed. They believed that no one owned the land. Can you think of one or more ways that people could have shared the land so that the families of the settlers and the Indians would have food, clothing, and shelter for their families and live together peacefully?

Something to Think About: Quotations

Quotations from Indian people who lived in the terrible times are interesting to read and to talk about. These words tell us what leaders believed, valued, and what they wanted in the future. You can just read and think about them or you could talk about them with your friends or family, or you could even write a letter to them and share your thoughts.

in Oregon. After gold was discovered in California in 1848, the Oregon Trail was as crowded as today's busy highway!

As the traders, miners, settlers and soldiers traveled along the Santa Fe Trail and Oregon Trail, they used the natural resources that the Indian people needed to live. They cut down trees and burned the wood in their campfires and killed the buffalo and other animals for their food and for their hides. Their horses and oxen ate the grasses needed by the Indians to graze their horses. Indian homelands and campsites were being destroyed by the travelers along the trails.

The people traveling along the trails also spread measles, smallpox, whooping cough, and especially **cholera**, to the Indians. These diseases killed many Indian people.

Most of the leaders of the Colorado tribes were angry but they tried to keep the peace. But, some of the young

Indians began to attack the wagon trains. Sometimes they would steal animals to feed their starving families.

The government wanted to work out a plan that would protect the travelers and be fair to the Indians. So they chose Thomas Fitzpatrick, who was a famous mountain man, to make a **treaty** with the Plains tribes.

In September 1851, about ten thousand Indians gathered together at Fort Laramie in what is now Wyoming. The Cheyenne, Arapaho, Lakota, Dakota, and Nakota Sioux, Crow, Shoshone and other Plains tribes met with government men for 18 days. They signed a treaty that pledged "lasting peace between all the nations **assembled**."

The government promised to protect the tribes from the actions that destroyed their grazing lands and killed the buffalo. They also promised that $50,000 worth of flour, sugar, rice, beef, coffee, cloth, and other things the Indians

"All we ask is that we may have peace with the whites. We want to take good tidings home to our people, that they may sleep in peace. I want you to give all the chiefs of the soldiers here to understand that we are for peace, and that we have made peace, that we may not be mistaken by them for enemies."
Chief Black Kettle, Southern Cheyenne

SOURCE: Miller, Lee. From the Heart: Voices of the American Indian. New York, NY: Alfred Knopf, 1995. p. 219.

"Great Father, I thank the Great Spirit, the Sun and the Moon, for putting me on this earth. It is a good earth, and I hope there will be no more fighting on it—that the grass will grow and the water fall, and plenty of buffalo. You, Grand Father, are doing well for your children, in coming so far and taking so much trouble about them. I think you will do us much good; I will go home satisfied. I will sleep sound, and not have to watch my horses in the night, nor be afraid for my [family]. We have to live on these streams and in the hills, and I would be glad if the whites would pick out a place for themselves and not come into our ground; but if they must pass through out country, they should give us game for what they drive off."
Chief Cut Nose (Southern Arapaho) - speaking after Fort Laramie Treaty

SOURCE: Trenhold, Virginia Cole. The Arapahoes, Our People (Reprint). Norman, OK : University of Oklahoma., 1986. p. 136.

needed would be given to them every year for fifty years. They promised that Southern Arapahoes and Cheyennes could keep their land between the Arkansas and Platte rivers and east into Kansas. The Indians promised they would not bother people traveling along the trails. They agreed that the government could build roads and military posts. Everyone left Ft. Laramie happy about the treaty.

Chief White Antelope

Even though the Indians were beginning to starve, the government broke their promise to give them food for 50 years. Usually the food was late; sometimes it was spoiled. The people traveling along the trails continued to break up and kill buffalo herds and use all the grass and wood. The Cheyenne, Arapaho, and the Sioux were hungry. Their horses were ridden so far to find food that they were in poor condition. Nearly half the Cheyenne and Arapaho died from cholera. Some warriors stole animals to feed their starving families. Others began to attack travelers on the Oregon Trail. The treaty of Fort Laramie did not work!

Who Discovered Gold in Colorado?

The men who discovered gold in Colorado were Indians. Two Cherokee and one Delaware man discovered gold in Colorado when they were on their way to California.

In 1853, when gold was discovered in Colorado, many of the miners who did not find gold in California came back to Colorado. About 50,000 people from the East and West poured into Colorado to look for gold. Towns like Denver were built on land that belonged to the Indians.

Chief Black Kettle

This was the land that was promised to them in the Fort Laramie Treaty. Many Indians camped and hunted around Denver and in the foothills. Toll roads were built to get miners to the mountains quicker and safer. The towns and roads were on Indian lands. The more land and resources the Indian people lost, the more desperate they were.

There were more and more Indian raids. Cheyenne and Arapaho leaders like Black Kettle and White Antelope (Cheyenne) and Left Hand and Little Raven (Southern Arapaho) worked hard for peace. They wanted their women and children to be safe.

John Evans was the second governor of the Colorado Territory. He was worried about the Indians who were desperate and beginning to fight to save their people. He thought he needed to protect the settlers and their property. The army bought William Bent's Big Timbers Fort and named it Fort Wise.

Governor Evans made a new treaty with the Indians. It was called The Fort Wise Treaty. It was signed by Cheyenne and Arapaho leaders. This treaty would give the Southern Cheyennes and Southern

Chief Little Raven

Chief Left Hand Bear

Arapahos a small reservation in Eastern Colorado. They were supposed to give up the rest of their land. But, they did not want to move to this new reservation because there were no buffalo there. Only one family moved. The rest continued to hunt along the Arkansas River. This made Governor Evans angry.

Chief Black Kettle and Chief Left Hand traveled to Denver to tell Governor Evans that they wanted peace. The governor would not meet with them. He ordered the "friendly" Indians to go to Fort Lyon. When these starving Indians got to Fort Lyon, they were told go to Sand Creek because there was no food for them at the fort. Evans also told Colonel John Chivington where the Indians would be camped. Chivington was eager to win an Indian battle.

About five Southern Cheyenne bands and ten Southern Arapaho lodges camped at Sand Creek. Black Kettle, Left Hand, and others were told that they would be safe there. They also were told to send the young warriors out to hunt because winter was coming soon. After the men left to find food, only women, children, and old men were in the camp. Colonel Chivington led an army of 700 men, out of Fort Lyon to Sand Creek. Their goal was to kill Indians.

On the morning of November 29, 1864, when Chief Black Kettle

> "Cheyennes will have to be soundly whipped before they will be quiet. If any of them are caught in your vicinity kill them, as that is the only way."
>
> Colonel John Chivington, United States Army.
>
> SOURCE: *Miller, Lee.* From the Heart: Voices of the American Indian. *New York, NY: Alfred Knopf, 1995. p. 219.*

saw the soldiers coming, he raised a large American flag and a white flag of peace. He thought that the attack was a mistake. Soon, Chief White Antelope knew that it was hopeless. He folded his arms, stood tall, and sang the Cheyenne Death Song. The words of the song are, " Nothing lives long, only the earth and the mountains." About 150 Cheyenne and Arapaho people were killed by Colonel John Chivington's soldiers. Mostly women and children were killed.

A skin painting of the Sand Creek Massacre. Can you see Chief Black Kettle?

George Bent Tells About Sand Creek

George Bent was the son of William Bent who built Bent's Fort in 1833. George's mother was a Cheyenne woman. Her name was Owl Woman. George was camped at Sand Creek on November 28, 1864. George was wounded, but he recovered. After Sand Creek, he fought with the Indians against the Americans.

When he was older, he wrote about his life. This is what happened to him at Sand Creek.

"This was the worst night I ever went through. There we were on that bleak, frozen plain without any shelter whatever and not a stick of wood to build a fire with. Most of us were wounded and half naked. Even those who had had time to dress when the attack came, had lost their buffalo robes and blankets during the fight. The men and women who were not wounded worked all through the night, trying to keep the children and the wounded from freezing to death. They gathered grass by the handful, feeding little fires around which the wounded and the children lay; they stripped off their own blankets and clothes to keep us warm. Some of the wounded who could not be provided with other covering were buried under piles of grass which their friends gathered, a handful at a time, and heaped up over them That night will never be forgotten as long as any of us who went through it are alive. It was bitter cold, the wind had a full sweep over the ground on which we lay, and in spite of everything that was done, no one could keep warm. All through the night the Indians kept hallooing [shouting] to attract the attention of those who had escaped from the village to the open plain and were wandering about in the dark, lost and freezing. Few were found alive, for the soldiers had done their work thoroughly. At last we could stand the cold no longer, and although it was still pitch-dark and long before dawn, we left that place and started east, where we knew Indians were encamped."

SOURCE: Hyde, George E. & Savoie Lottinville (ed.). Life of George Bent Written From His Letters. Norman, OK: University of Oklahoma 1968. pp. 157-158.

The soldiers came back to Denver and marched in a parade to celebrate their victory. Soon, people in Colorado and other parts of the United States began to find out more about the **incident**. Many of these people thought it was not a victory, but a **massacre** instead. A massacre is when people are attacked and killed when they aren't able to fight back. They wanted Congress to find out if

Capt. S. S. Soule

Sand Creek was a victory or a massacre.

Captain Silas S. Soule, who was Commander of Cavalry Company D, would not let his soldiers shoot at the Indians. He told the Congress what really happened. Soon after that, he was shot outside his home. His killer was never punished. Congress decided that the attack at Sand Creek had been a terrible act against a peaceful village. It was a massacre.

What happened at Sand Creek was the beginning of Indian wars across the Plains. Because of Sand Creek, Governor Evans was asked to **resign**. Colonel Chivington retired from the army so that he wouldn't be punished.

About three years after the Sand Creek Massacre, another treaty was signed by the Comanche, Kiowa,

"It will be a very hard thing to leave the country that God gave us. Our friends are buried there, and we hate to leave these grounds. There at Sand Creek White Antelope, and many other chiefs lie there; our women and children lie there. Our lodges were destroyed there, and our horses were taken from us."

Chief Little Raven

Cruel Waste

In 1857, U.S. soldiers were ordered to destroy a Cheyenne village. About 20,000 pounds of buffalo meat was destroyed. This meat was supposed to feed the whole village that winter.

SOURCE: Crum, Sally. *People of the Red Earth. Santa Fe, NM: Ancient City Press,* 1996. *p. 108.*

Kiowa-Apache, Cheyenne, and Arapaho. It was called the Medicine Lodge Treaty. The government promised food, clothing, farm equipment, some guns for hunting, and teachers for the

Indians for the next 30 years. The Indians agreed to stay on small reservations in Kansas and Oklahoma, not to stop the building of the railroads and not to harm the settlers or their property. Colorado was no longer the homelands of the Cheyenne and Arapaho.

George Bent said that this was the most important treaty ever signed by the Cheyennes. It was the beginning of the end of the Cheyenne people as free warriors and hunters. (Bent, p. 285)

"Kill every buffalo you can. Every buffalo dead is an Indian gone." Colonel R. I. Dodge, United States Army.

SOURCE: Miller, Lee. From the Heart: Voices of the American Indian. New York, NY: Alfred Knopf, 1995. p. 228.

The Union Pacific Railroad that went across America was finished in 1869. The railroad went through southern Wyoming. It divided the buffalo on the Plains into two herds. The southern herd of buffalo on Colorado's plains were **slaughtered**

A mountain of buffalo skulls, ca. 1870

by hunters between 1871 and 1874. The hunters killed them for their hides and for sport. They left the bodies to rot in the sun. Sometimes the hunters just took the tongues of the buffalo to eat. In ten years, the northern herd had been slaughtered too. Without the buffalo on the plains, there was little food for the Indians; they needed the buffalo to survive. Killing all of the buffalo was a war on Indian people.

After the Sand Creek massacre, there were many battles across the Plains. The angry Indians came together to fight for their families and homelands. In 1876, the Indians won one large battle called the Battle of the Bighorn. The last battle was the battle of Wounded Knee in 1890. When the battles were over. the Indians lost much of the

Colorado Statehood

On August 1, 1876 Colorado became a state. There were about 100,000 people who lived in Colorado. The Indians were not counted.

land they called home. The Indians of the Plains were forced to live on reservations in many nearby states. The Southern Cheyenne and the Southern Arapaho now live on a reservation in Oklahoma. The Northern Arapaho with the Shoshone live on the Wind River Reservation in Wyoming. The Northern Cheyenne now live on a reservation in Montana.

Grandmother quietly finished telling her story. She found a map and showed Grace where the reservations were on the map. The Cheyenne and Arapaho did survive the terrible times. Like all people, they have changed over time. But their people and their traditions are alive.

The Rest of the Story

The wars were over. But, there were other kinds of battles that lasted for a very long time. These battles were about Indian beliefs, values, and lifeways. The United

> **U.S. Treaties**
>
> In 1870 the United States stopped making treaties with the Indians. Instead, they made laws for Indians to follow. This **policy** did not care about what Indians wanted or needed.

States government tried to wipe out Indian language, religions, and cultures. They wanted the Indians to forget being Indian and be like other Americans instead.

When Indian people were moved to reservations, the government wanted them to own small pieces of land called **allotments**. The Indian people did not understand. They always believed the land belonged to everyone. Soon most of Indian land had owners but usually those owners were not Indian. Much Indian land was lost to people who were not Indian.

The government wanted Indian men to farm these allotments. The men thought growing food was the work done by women, not men and they did not want to be farmers. Many allotments were dry land and not good for farming. The allotments did not work out well.

Indian children were forced to go to government or church schools, cut their long hair, wear "American" clothes, and speak only English. The schools often taught children that their Indian languages and cultures were bad. The government and the churches wanted Indian people to forget their traditional dances and ceremonies and learn new religions. Traditional Indian ceremonies and dances were not allowed.

This too was a terrible time for Indian families. But Indian languages and lifeways are strong. They continue today and Indian families are becoming strong again. In the next chapters, you will learn how Indian beliefs, values, and traditions continue today.

Timeline of Events in the Terrible Times

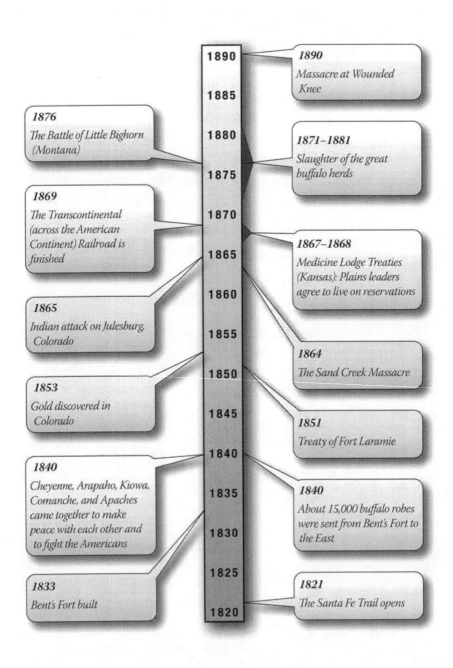

1890
Massacre at Wounded Knee

1876
The Battle of Little Bighorn (Montana)

1871–1881
Slaughter of the great buffalo herds

1869
The Transcontinental (across the American Continent) Railroad is finished

1867–1868
Medicine Lodge Treaties (Kansas): Plains leaders agree to live on reservations

1865
Indian attack on Julesburg, Colorado

1864
The Sand Creek Massacre

1853
Gold discovered in Colorado

1851
Treaty of Fort Laramie

1840
Cheyenne, Arapaho, Kiowa, Comanche, and Apaches came together to make peace with each other and to fight the Americans

1840
About 15,000 buffalo robes were sent from Bent's Fort to the East

1833
Bent's Fort built

1821
The Santa Fe Trail opens

Timeline scale: 1820, 1825, 1830, 1835, 1840, 1845, 1850, 1855, 1860, 1865, 1870, 1875, 1880, 1885, 1890

More Books to Read:

Bunting, Eve. *Cheyenne Again*. New York, NY: Clarion, 1995.

Finley, Mary Peace. *Little Fox's Secret: The Mystery of Bent's Fort*. Palmer Lake, CO: Filter Press, 1999.

Goble, Paul. *Death of the Iron Horse*. New York, NY: Bradbury, 1987.

Grumman, Jewell Gay Matthaei. *The Ledgerbook of Thomas Blue Eagle*. Charlottesville, VA: Thomasson-Grant, 1994.

Isaacs, Sally Senzell. *Life on the Oregon Trail*. Chicago, IL: Heinemann, 2000.

Videos/DVDs to Watch:

Schlessinger, Andrew (Producer). *Daily Pioneer Life*. Wynnewood, PA: Schlessinger, 2004.

Schlessinger, Andrew (Producer). *The Pioneer Journey Westward*. Wynnewood, PA: Schlessinger, 2004.

Schlessinger, Andrew (Producer). *Westward Expansion in the U. S.* Wynnewood, PA: Schlessinger, 2004.

SOURCE: *www.libraryvideo.com* (This site has many appropriate videos/DVDs)

Places to Go:

Bent's Old Fort

35110 Highway 194 East
La Junta, CO 81050-9523

OR

40 Santa Fe
La Junta, CO 81050
Phone:719-383-5010

Flying J Ranch Park

This park is off Highway 73, between Conifer and Evergreen in Jefferson County. This park is on land that was part of Cheyenne, Arapaho, and Ute hunting grounds. When roads were built into the mountains during the Gold Rush, two of them, the Mount Vernon Toll Road and the Denver, Bradford and Blue River road met at the present junction of Highway 73 and Barkley Road, opposite the park property. Take a nice hike in the park and imagine what it would have been like in the 1800s.

Websites to Visit:

Bent's Old Fort http://www.nps.gov/beo/html

Santa Fe Trail http:// www.rmpbs.org/byways/sft_intro.html

Sand Creek Massacre http:// www.sandcreek.org

Request for Governor Evans' resignation
        http://www.colorado.gov/dpa/doit/archives/evans/ff9.htm

Things to Do

Colorado Counties with Historical Names

On a map of Colorado, find Arapahoe County, Bent County, Cheyenne County, Kiowa County. and Ouray County.

Life on the Oregon Trail

Read *Life on the Oregon Trail* by Sally Senzell Isaacs. Can you find pioneer activities in the book that were harmful for Indian people? Did the people know that they were disturbing Indian lifeways? Explain your answers.

Our Ancestors

Kara is in the fifth grade. She is not Indian. She is learning about her ancestors that lived in the 1800s. Can you find the names of your ancestors who lived in the 1840s? Did they live in Colorado? Were they Indian people? Were they settlers? What countries did they come from? Does your family have old photographs of your ancestors? These are Kara's grandmothers on her mother's side of her family. Kara is the granddaughter of the author of this book!

Kara's Genealogy

Name	Birth Year	Relationship
Kara Michelle Eikermann	1999	child
Kelsey Lynn Harvey	1962	mother
Karen Ann Decker	1935	grandmother
Sarah Constance Herndon	1908	great grandmother
Nina Margaret Smith	1881	great-great grandmother
Anna Rebecca O'Neil	1860	great-great-great grandmother
Anna Hennessy	1824	great-great-great-great grand mother

Anna Hennessy, her daughter, and her granddaughter lived in the 1800s. In 1876, Colorado became a state.

Ledgerbooks

Learn more about ledgerbooks.

Afton, Jean, Halaas, David Fridtjof, and Andrew E. Masich. *Cheyenne Dog Soldiers: A Ledgerbook History of Coups and Combat.* University Press of Colorado: Niwot, CO and Colorado Historical Society: Boulder, CO, 1997.

Can you think of an important incident or event that you could record by drawing in a ledgerbook or tablet? You will need lots of details to tell a good story!

Definitions

Allotment	a 160 acre piece of land given to someone to farm
Assembled	gathered together
Bale	a kind of package held together by wire or rope
Banned	not allowed
Cholera	a disease that causes severe diarrhea and often death
Incident	an action or situation that is likely to have a bad effect
Ledgerbook	a small book with lined pages that Indian people got from Americans and used to draw pictures that recorded events in their history
Massacre	the killing of a large number of defenseless people
Negotiate	to try to reach an agreement by discussion and compromise
Pioneer	the first non-Indian people to settle in a territory
Policy	a government plan of action
Resign	to give up your job or position
Slaughter	to kill in large numbers
Starve	to suffer or die from not having enough food
Treaty	a written agreement between two countries
U.S. Treaties	legal agreements

Terrible Times and Change for the Utes

Like the Cheyenne and Arapaho, the stories of the Utes are remembered and told to the children by the grandmothers and grandfathers. But Eddie, who lives on the Southern Ute Reservation, is very lucky. He has many ways to learn the history of his people. Because he lives on the Southern Ute Reservation, he goes to a Ute School. It is called the Southern Ute Indian Montessori Academy. The Ute name for the school is *Pinunuuchi Pöögani*. At school, he learns Ute history and language from his Ute teachers and elders.

Many of the old stories which have been told by the elders are written now, so he learns by reading too. Some stories have been saved on the computer! It is important to the Ute people that their children learn about Ute culture and history. This is one of the reasons that the Southern Ute created their own school. At school, Eddie and other children learn about their Ute people and how their lives were changed when the Europeans and Americans came to their lands. This is part of their history.

The Story of the Utes

Long ago, the Utes were enemies of the Cheyenne and Arapaho. They raided each other's villages and hunting grounds. But their struggles to save their lands and cultures were much the same. The stories about what happened to the Utes' homelands and traditional ways of life are very much like the stories about what happened to the Cheyenne and Arapaho people.

This was a time in United States history when most Americans believed in Manifest Destiny. This was a belief that the United States had the right to spread their government, their religions, and their lifeways across North America, by force if necessary.

Americans thought that this would be good for everybody, including the Indians that lived there.

They thought the Indians and their cultures were blocking the growth of America. They didn't understand why Indians loved their land, their languages, their values, and their traditions and didn't want give up their ways of life. This was the belief or policy that created the terrible times for Indian people.

The Utes were safe for a long time. Their traditional tribal lands and hunting grounds covered more than half of Colorado, almost half of Utah, and parts of northern New Mexico and southern Wyoming (*map, page 45*). The high mountains protected them from intruders in many ways. But valuable gold and silver were discovered below the ground in the shining mountains. The parks and valleys were good for ranching too. The newcomers wanted this Ute land for mining and ranches. There were strong Ute leaders who worked for peace but they were not successful. The miners and settlers wanted their land and they took it!

In the beginning, the Utes were friendly toward new people. Some of the first white men in the mountains were from Spain. The Utes helped them them find their way through the mountains to California. In the 1830s and 1840s Spanish traders brought wool serapes, kettles, knives, and other things to trade with the Utes. Fur trappers also came into Ute territory.

After Columbus landed, Spanish explorers claimed the land that is now Mexico for Spain. Then in 1824, the people who lived on that land fought Spain for their freedom. They wanted to be an independent country. This new country was called Mexico and it was much larger than it is now. Then, in 1848, at the end of the Mexican-American War, the United States took all of the Mexican land that was in North America. This land is now California, Arizona, Utah, Nevada, and parts of Wyoming, Colorado, and New

Mexico. Suddenly, many Spanish and Mexican citizens were citizens of the United States!

For many years the Spanish and Mexican governments gave a lot of traditional Ute land to their citizens, especially in the San Luis Valley and around the Arkansas River. These settlers built farms on the Utes' favorite hunting grounds. They plowed up the land where Utes dug for roots. They killed the game that the Utes used for food and clothing. The land that the Utes could use to find what they needed to survive kept getting smaller and smaller.

Soon, a United States fort was built to protect the settlers. It was called Fort Massachusetts. The building of the fort frightened the Utes and made them angry. The Utes fought back with raids on the settlers. Later Fort Massachusetts was moved six miles away and named Fort Garland. It was very hard to keep the peace during this time.

The Utes lived in seven bands. Three bands, the *Mouache, Capote,* and *Weeminuches*, were called the **Southern Utes**. The other four bands, the *Uncompahgre* (*Tabeguache*), *Yampa, White River,* and *Grand River* Utes were called the **Northern Utes**. Each band had its own leader. The United States government wanted to work with only one leader. So they named Ouray as chief of the Utes. Ouray was a Northern Ute and the leader of the Uncompahgre band. The other bands were angry that Ouray was the man chosen to speak for all bands. When he signed treaties for the Utes, many of the Southern

Some Important Ute Leaders

- Colorow *ca.* 1810–1888 (Northern Ute–White River)
- Jack House 1887?–1971 (Southern Ute–Weeminuche)
- Ignacio 1828–1913 (Southern Ute–Weeminuche)
- Nicaagat (or Jack) *fl.* 1870s (Northern Ute–White River
- Ouray ca. 1820–1880 (Northern Ute-Tabeguache)

Ute people didn't think that he spoke for them. This was a problem!

Ouray was a good leader. He spoke English, Spanish, Ute, and some Apache. Ouray knew that the United States had many more people, horses, soldiers, and guns than the Utes. He also knew the Utes would not be able to win a war against the United States. He wanted the Utes to be paid for the land that they had to give up. He thought his people would be safer on a protected reservation. He worked to make sure that the Utes kept the best of their land.

> "Agreements the Indian makes with the government are like the agreement a buffalo makes with the hunter after it has been pierced by many arrows. All it can do is lie down and give in.
>
> We shall fall as the leaves from the trees when frost or winter comes, and the lands which we have roamed over for countless generations will be given over to the miner and the plowshare *(farmers' plow)*, and we shall be buried out of sight beneath the avalanche of the new civilization.
>
> We do not want to sell a foot of our land. That is the opinion of all."
>
> Chief Ouray
>
> SOURCE: *Miller, Lee (Ed.).* From the Heart. *New York, NY: Alfred A. Knopf, 1995. pp. 287-288.*

Ouray and Chipeta

Ouray, Chipeta and the Ute Chiefs in Washington

With ten Ute chiefs and his beautiful wife, Chipeta, Ouray went to Washington to negotiate the Treaty of 1868. In Washington, they met President Andrew Johnson, visited the museums and government buildings, and saw the sights of this beautiful city. In this treaty, the Utes lost the San Luis Valley and much of the Rocky Mountains. The treaty also gave about one-third of western Colorado to the Utes. This was about 16,500,000 acres. No white man was allowed to enter this land without permission from the Utes.

The new treaty also promised that the government would give each Ute family 160 acres of land, farm tools, and seeds to plant. They promised that people would teach them how to be farmers. There would be two Indian agencies or government offices established, one for the Northern Utes and one for the Southern Utes.

In this treaty, the agencies would have teachers, farmers, and blacksmiths, and each family would get a cow and five sheep to get their farms started. The treaty promised that the United States government would build schools for the Ute children who wanted to go to school. The seven bands were promised $30,000 each year in clothing, blankets, and other things they needed. They were also promised $30,000 in meat, wheat, flour, beans, and potatoes until the people could grow enough crops to feed themselves. The seven bands were supposed to have their fair share of everything.

The Treaty of 1868 also gave Ouray $1,000 a year for life because he helped the government get other Utes to sign the treaty. The Southern Utes did not like that!

Very quickly, the settlers and miners decided that the land the Utes received in the treaty was too valuable for a bunch of Indians. They thought that the Utes had too much of the land that they needed and wanted. They believed that when the Utes learned to be farmers, they would not need all of the land anyway. They didn't like the treaty.

An Indian agent said that the Utes were good neighbors to the miners. They often fed and helped them. But the miners didn't pay any attention to the treaty. They continued to mine in the San Juan mountains which was Ute land. The army had a very hard time trying to remove the miners.

Wovoka

The Piute are closely related to the Ute and lived in the Great Basin Culture Area. Wovoka, who was a Piute leader, said this to his people.

"My people, before the white man came you were happy. You had many buffalo to eat and tall grass for your ponies—you could come and go like the wind. When it grew cold you could journey to the valleys of the south, where healing springs are; and when it grew warm, you could return to the mountains of the north. The white man came. He dug up the bones of our mother, the earth. He tore her bosom with steel. He built big trails and put iron horses on them. He fought you and beat you, and put you in barren places where a horned toad would die. He said you must stay there; you must not go hunt in the mountains."

SOURCE: Vanderwerth, W. C. (comp). Indian Oratory: Famous Speeches by Noted Indian Chieftains (6th ed.). Norman, OK: University of Oklahoma, 1989. p. 129.

The Utes didn't like the treaty either. As it turned out, many of the Indian agents were dishonest. People didn't get the promised food and when they did it was often rotten. The wild cows escaped!

Ouray was unhappy that the Treaty of 1868 was not honored. Still he did not want to sell this land. Ouray knew that the Utes could not win a war. So, he and other leaders went to Washington again. Finally, the Utes agreed to sell the rich mining area in the San Juan mountains. This sale was called the Brunot Agreement. They lost one-fourth of their reservation. The Utes were supposed to get $25,000 each year forever. Ouray was given $1,000 a year for ten years as long as he was the leader of the Utes and at peace with the government.

Soon there was trouble again. The government didn't honor their promises to the Utes. Now, many of the Ute bands blamed Ouray for giving up their land.

A new Indian agent, Nathan Meeker, was sent to the White River Agency. The agency was in the land of the Northern Utes who lived and hunted around the Yampa, Grand, and White Rivers. It was far away from any settlers. Meeker's goal was to make the Utes into hard working farmers. He had no training in farming and did not respect Indian cultures.

Meeker moved the agency to a new place four miles away. The agency was now near a rich horse grazing pasture. Then he ordered

Nathan Meeker

the pasture plowed up so that garden crops could be planted. He didn't want the Utes to stop working on the farm, so he made them come to the agency each week for the food that had been promised to them in the treaties.

An Indian leader named Johnson, who owned many horses, was very angry about the plowing. He went to Meeker's office. Meeker told him he owned too many horses. Johnson pushed him down. Meeker was frightened so he sent a telegram to the government saying that he and his family were not safe. He wanted government troops to come to the agency. Remember that the treaties did not allow others on Ute land without their permission.

Major T. T. Thornburg began to march about 150 troops from Fort Steele in Wyoming to the White River Agency. Traders warned their Indian friends. When the troops entered Ute land they were surrounded by Ute warriors. A shot rang out! Major Thornburg was killed.

Back at the agency, Meeker, and nine other people were killed by a few Utes. Mrs. Meeker, her daughter Josephine, and another woman with two children were carried away by the Utes from the agency to where the Ute women and children were staying.

By now Ouray was told about the trouble at the agency and quickly he was on his way to help. Ouray arranged to have the women and children set free. They said that they had been treated well. Later, the women changed their story and helped to turn Colorado settlers against the Utes.

The Meeker incident was the end of the Ute's long fight for freedom. People who wanted to settle on Ute lands used many ways to make the settlers afraid of the Ute. The motto in a Denver newspaper was "The Utes Must Go!"

> "There is no use of making a long ado about the Indian question, the only solution of the problem is extermination."
>
> The *Colorado Banner*, an early newspaper
>
> SOURCE: Miller, Lee (Ed.). From the Heart. *New York, NY: Alfred A. Knopf, 1995. p. 288.*

Reproduction of a sketch of the Meeker incident at the White River Ute Indian Agency, September 29th 1879, Rio Blanco County, Colorado, shows soldiers surveying the destruction from the fire and battle between Native American Utes and Nathan Meeker and his employees.

The caption under the picture reads: "(A) piles of ashes, (F) the Agency Farm, (G) graves of the Agent and employees where they fell, (J) house of Sub-Chief Johnson, (M) grave of Indian Agent Meeker, (P) grave of Post, the Clerk and Postmaster."

Gravestones read: "N. C. Meeker, Agt. White River, Utes, Killed By Them, Sept. 29 or 30," and "W. H. Post, Clerk Agt. Killed By Utes, Sept. 29, 30, 31, 1879." Source: Printed in Frank Leslie's Illustrated Newspaper on December 6, 1879, p. 245. Author: Lieutenant C. A. H. McCauley, Third U. S. Cavalry (Note: McCauley died in 1913.)

After 1879, the government told the Northern Utes to go to Grand Junction. From there they were forced to leave their shining mountains and valleys and walk to a desert-like reservation in Utah. This was the Uintah Reservation. It was later called the Uintah-Ouray Reservation. The non-Indians in New Mexico and Colorado wanted the Southern Utes moved to Utah. The non-Indians in Utah didn't want them there. Everyone thought the Utes must go!

Finally, the Southern Utes were went to a small reservation in southwestern Colorado in 1880. It was about 110 miles long and 15 miles wide.

Now, the only Indians who lived on their homelands in Colorado were the Mouache, Capote, and Weeminuche Ute bands. In 1895, the government wanted to give each Ute family an allotment. Then when all of the families had their own piece of land, they would open the rest of the land to settlers that were not Indian.

Something to Think About

The Southern Utes voted on having allotments and 153 men voted for allotments and 148 voted against. If you voted for allotments, your family would own 160 acres. If you voted against, you and your family would live in the old way when the land belonged to everyone. If you were a Ute man, how would you vote? Why?

When the Utes voted on this law, 153 people voted for it and 148 voted against it. Only the men could vote. The Weeminuche people did not want to own an allotment. They wanted to live in the old way when the land belonged to everyone. So, Ignacio, a famous Weeminuche leader, and the Weeminuche band settled on a piece of the western end of the reservation and became the Ute Mountain Ute tribe. The Ute Mountain Ute Reservation also includes small parts of New Mexico and Utah. The land of the Southern Utes is called a "checkerboard" because some land is settled by Indians and some by non-Indians.

Now the Southern Utes and the Ute Mountain Utes are the only Indians who live on their homelands in Colorado!

The Story of Chipeta and Change

Chipeta was the wife of Ouray, a Tabegauche (Uncompahgre) leader who tried to save traditional Ute lands and cultures. Although the Tabegauche were moved to a reservation in Utah, Chipeta is honored in the history of Colorado. Her life is a story of love and kindness, happy and sad times, and old and new ways. She lived in a time that was very hard for Indian people. Change was happening all around her. She faced these changes and earned the respect of the Ute and American people.

Chipeta was born in about 1843. A Tabegauche hunting party heard a frightened child crying in a Kiowa-Apache camp. Everyone in the camp had been killed except this little girl. She was adopted by the the family of the Ute warrior who found and comforted her. Children who were alone like Chipeta often were adopted into Ute families.

Chipeta was small. Her nose was different and her face not as round and brown as the faces of Ute children. But she was raised in Ute traditions and she became a Ute, not a Kiowa-Apache, woman.

When she was about fifteen years old, she was chosen to take care of a baby whose mother had died. The father of the baby was a handsome man who was respected as a hunter and warrior. His name was Ouray. He needed someone to take care of his baby, Pahlone, and do the woman's work for him. Chipeta loved Pahlone. She was pretty, smart, and kind and soon she and Ouray were married in the Ute way. She was Ouray's partner and took care of the baby, Ouray, and their home.

Later, when Ouray became a chief, he was often be away from home. Chipeta visited the people in the camps to learn about their worries and the things they wanted and needed. Then she would tell everything she learned to Ouray after he came home. When he returned from trips to Washington where he met with the government and negotiated treaties, she visited the camps to tell the people what happened in Washington.

Chipeta welcomed many people to her home where they met to make tribal decisions or fix problems. In Ute life, women did not make decisions for the tribe. Tribal meetings were for men only. But, Ouray wanted her by his side. At first, the Utes didn't understand

and Chipeta was embarrassed when she went to tribal meetings. In time, the people learned to trust her and value her wisdom.

One day, her son Pahlone wandered from the Ute hunting camp. Ouray and the men searched for him for days, but they did not find him. Chipeta cried for the loss of her son. Years later, Pahlone was found. He had been adopted by the Arapaho who were enemies of the Ute. When Pahlone finally met Ouray, he said he hated the Utes. Ouray was very quiet. Then he said that Pahlone was not his son and walked away. Now Chipeta had lost her son forever. She never forgot Pahlone but, in the Ute way, she adopted other children to love and care for.

When she had to move from her home in Conejos Agency to the Los Pios Agency, she was sad. But she packed her things and made their home in this new place. Because the agency was located in a place that was too high and too cold, the agency was moved again to the Uncompahgre Valley after the Brunot Treaty was signed. This agency was called Los Pios II.

At the new agency, Ouray chose 160 acres and built a ranch. He wanted to show his people a new way of life. They planted crops and a garden and built a house. They didn't use the tipi except when they went on trips. Chipeta missed living in a tipi. But, she put rugs on the floor and curtains on the windows in her new house. The rooms had fireplaces and wood stoves for heat and oil lamps for light.

She bought iron beds, chairs, a dresser, a piano, and a large mirror. A big table was built. She received gifts of china, crystal, and silver. She used those when she had visitors that were not Indian. She still planted a garden and butchered meat. She visited the camps and was a part of the traditional Ute activities.

Ouray became very tired and sick. Still he worked with the government and the Utes to find peace. After the Meeker incident, people in Colorado wanted the Utes to leave the state. He made a trip to Washington to tell Congress what happened when Nathan

Meeker was killed. This time Chipeta went with him. She took her first train ride and learned about life in Washington. She even did some shopping in the big stores. But, she was used to her busy way of life in Colorado and did not like living in this strange world.

In Washington, Ouray worked on making a new treaty that both the Northern Utes and the Southern Utes needed to sign. Ouray helped the Ute people understand the treaty. When he got back to Colorado, he visited the Southern Ute Agency to explain the treaty and to ask them to sign it. He died on August 24, 1880, when he was visiting the Southern Ute Agency. He was buried in the Ute way two miles south of Ignacio.

Items Bought by Chipeta in Washington

- 8 yards of cloth for dresses
- 4 spools of cotton thread
- 1 1/2 yards of satin
- 3 spools of silk thread
- 2 3/4 yards of cambric
- 2 packages of needles
- 6 yards of plaid
- 1 1/2 dozen buttons
- 3 yards of flannel
- 1 skirt
- 15 yards of cotton
- 3 pair of hose
- 2 yards of twill
- 1 pair of gloves

She spent $27.00 which was paid by the government.

When the new treaty was signed by everyone, Chipeta was moved with the Taubegauche close to the Uintah reservation in Utah. The agency later was named the Unitah-Ouray Reservation. It was painful for her to leave the Colorado ranch that she loved. The trip was hard. Each family received enough beef, flour, hard bread, and salt for three weeks. They also got 600 pounds of sugar, 250 pounds of coffee, and 50 pounds of tobacco that the government owed them.

Chipeta now lived like everyone else on the reservation. Hunting and farming was hard on this land. It was cold too. The government said they would build her another house like her first house in Los

Pios II, but they built a two room cabin instead. They sold her furniture and the things in her house. She stood in line to get her annuities like everyone else did.

When she married again, she and her new husband adopted children who needed homes. She made trips to Colorado where she took part in parades and other celebrations. Once she went to a hospital in Grand Junction to have her eyes treated.

Chipeta died on August 16, 1924. She was eighty-one years old. Her brother McCook wrapped her body in a blanket and buried her in the Ute way. She was later reburied in Montrose in 1925.

Five thousand people came to this funeral to show their respect for her. A band played "America." She lived and died as a Ute.

Many events brought change in Chipeta's life. But her Indian values stayed strong and never changed. She was always modest, kind, generous, and loving. Her life was hard. She lost her son, Pahlone, her husband, Ouray, and the traditional homelands she loved. The world around her changed too. Cars, trains, hospitals, schools, churches, and farming were all new to her. There were new laws that shaped her life. Her Indian values helped to make her strong. She was respected by her people who showed their respect for her by calling her "Grandmother." She was also respected by the people of Colorado. The newspapers wrote about her and she was honored by many parades and gifts. Today she is remembered as a proud Indian woman of peace, love, and strength.

> **Something to Think About: Chipeta**
>
> In the last year's of Chipeta's life, she chose to live like all Utes on the reservation. She was poor, lived in a tipi, and ate government food (annuities). In many ways she was admired by the people in Colorado and could have chosen to live differently. Why do you think she chose to live on the reservation? Why do people honor her?

Timeline of the Terrible Times

1896
A new agency was set up for the Weeminuche who didn't want allotments

1899
Southern Ute Reservation was opened up to non-Indians

1900

1895
Ignacio led most of the Weeminuche to the western part of the Southern Ute Reservation because they did not agree with the policy of land allotment.

1895

1896
Allotments are given to the Southern Utes

1890

1895
The Southern Utes agree to the allotments

1886
The Uintah and Ouray Reservations joined together

1885

1889
The Ute Agreement was signed

1880
Reservation is created for Southern Utes, a 15 by 100 mile strip of land

1880

1881
The Tabeguache and White River bands moved to the Uintah Reservation in Utah

1875

1879
The Meeker Incident - Nathan Meeker is killed

1880
Chief Ouray dies

1870

1874
The Utes gave up the San Juan Mountain area in the Brunot Agreement

1877
The Southern Ute Agency was established at Ignacio for the Capotes, Mouaches, and Weeminuche bands

1865

1873
Gold and silver rush in the San Juan Mountains

1868
Treaty of 1868 moves Utes to ⅓ of the western part of Colorado

1860

1861
Territory of Colorado was created

1858
Fort Massachusetts was moved and renamed Fort Garland.

1855

1851-1853
People who had been Mexican citizens began to settle in the San Luis Valley

1852
Fort Massachusetts was built.

1850

1848
Gold is discovered in California

1845

1848
Treaty of Guadalupe Hidalgo that ended the Mexican-American War

More Books to Read

Flanagan, Alice K. *The Utes*. New York, NY: Children's Press, 1998.

Krudwig, Vickie Leigh. *Searching for Chipeta*. Golden, CO: Fulcrum, 2004.

Wyss, Thelma Hatch. *Bear Dancer*. New York, NY: Margaret K. McElderry Books, 2005.

Videos/DVDs to Watch

Anderson, P. (Producer). *Ute Legacy*. Ignacio, CO: Southern Ute Tribe/ Colorado Historical Society, 1999.

Places to Go

Fort Garland Museum
Fort Garland, CO 81133
Telephone: 719-379-3512

The Ute Indian Museum & Ouray Memorial Park
17253 Chipeta Drive
Montrose, Colorado 81401
Telephone: 970-249-3098

Southern Ute Cultural Center and Museum
77 County Road 517
Ignacio, CO
Telephone: 970-563-9583

Websvites to Visit

Ute Mountain Ute: http://www.utemountainute.com/

Southern Ute: http://www.southern-ute.nsn.us/

Things to Do

Make a Poster
Make a poster for one of these mottos:
The Utes Must Stay   *Or*   This is Ute Land

Definitions

Acre   an acre is 4840 square yards with 640 acres in a square mile

Agency   an official United States government office on Indian reservations

Annuities	the food, tools, and other goods promised to the Indians in the treaties
Claim	to say something belongs to you
fl.	the high point of a person's life or career when his/her dates of birth are unknown
Intrude	to enter without invitation, permission, or welcome
Manifest Destiny	the belief in the 1840s that the United States should expand or spread across the continent, by force if necessary
Motto	a short way of communicating the meaning of an idea

Chapter 8
Life Today for Colorado Indians

At Indian Club, Grace and her friends are learning how to cook some traditional Indian foods. In the beginning, it was going to be one lesson but now they are planning six cooking lessons - and maybe more! Grace is Southern Cheyenne, John is Osage, Mary and Tina are Lakota, Bill, David, and Lucille are Dine´ (Navajo), Margaret is Ojibwe, Charlie is Ute, and Valerie is Pawnee. The other kids are from many other tribes and culture areas. Many of her friends who come to Indian Club are mixed blood Indians. That means that their mother (or a grandmother) may be from one tribe and their father (or a grandfather) from another tribe. Or, one or more of their parents or grandparents may not be Indian at all.

There is not one "traditional" Indian food and each tribe has their own special foods. Tribes from different culture areas have

special traditional foods and ways of preparing them. So, Grace and her friends are going to cook the traditional foods of many Indian nations. Wild rice, mutton stew, turkey, corn, beans, cranberries, squash, pine nuts, salmon, and sassafras tea, are some of the traditional foods of American Indian tribes.

Grace is hungry already! She is excited to learn to cook outside in traditional ways. Traditional cooking is a little like camping and she loves to camp. They have already decided that they need some adults to help them, especially if they build a fire outside or dig a pit to cook foods in the old ways. But traditional foods are prepared in modern ways too! It will be fun to learn the old ways of cooking, but the new ways are a lot easier.

As always, Grace now has many new questions. There were many Indian children in her school. Has anyone lived on a reservation? Why did their families come from all parts of the country to live in Denver? Do they go to their reservations to visit relatives or for important ceremonies? Do their families still eat traditional foods? Do they fix traditional food in old or new ways? Do the Indian families in Denver or other **urban** areas live differently than the families on the Southern Ute Reservation and Ute Mountain Reservation?

Grace wants to make a recipe book of the foods they learn about. They will have lots of fun cooking and eating different traditional Indian foods and they will learn more about how Indian families lived in the past and today too.

Because Grace is Southern Cheyenne and lives in Denver and the Southern Cheyenne reservation is in Oklahoma, she doesn't know very much about reservation life. She wants to learn more about family life on the Ute reservations in Colorado. She is curious about how many Indian people live in Colorado. How many live on the reservations? How many live in Denver, Boulder, Grand Junction, and Colorado Springs?

One way to find some of the answers to Grace's questions is to study the 2000 **Census** which will tell us how many Indians lived in Colorado in 2000. First, it is important to understand that even if the census is supposed to count every person in the country every ten years, it still isn't a perfect count. Some people don't want to be counted. Some people don't give correct information. It is possible for someone to say that they are Indian when they are not. Mixed blood people are counted in a different way. But even if the census isn't perfect, it still gives us important information.

The Six Colorado Counties with the Most Indians in 2000	
1. Denver	7,290
2. El Paso	4,725
3. Adams	4,321
4. Jefferson	3,971
5. Arapahoe	3,234
6. Montezuma	2,676

Beginning with the 2000 census, people could say that they belonged to just one race or more than one. This was not possible in the 1990 census. So it is hard to compare the information from the 2000 and 2010 census with the 1990 census.

Colorado Population Distribution by Census Year

Year	Total Population	Native American Population	Native American % of Total	Mixed Descent Population	Mixed Descent % of Total
1990	3,294,394	27,776	0.84%		
2000	4,301,261	44,241	1.03%	122,187	2.84%
2010	5,029,196	56,010	1.11%	172,456	3.43%

Now, lets look at the 2000 census on the two Colorado reservations. Not all of the Indian people are Utes and some are not Indian.

Reservation Population Distribution by Census Year

Reservation	Total Population		Native American Population		Native American % of Total		Mixed Descent Population		Mixed Descent % of Total	
Year	2000	2010	2000	2010	2000	2010	2000	2010	2000	2010
Southern Ute	11,159	12,153	1,433	1,388	12.8%	11.4%	354	355	3.2%	2.9%
Ute Mountain Ute & off-reservation trust land	1,410	1,500	1,337	1,430	94.8%	95.3%	38	38	2.7%	2.5%

This is what Census 2010 tells us about Indian people who live in Colorado today.

- ◼ American Indian people live in Colorado's urban, **rural**, and reservation areas.
- ◼ There are Indian people living in all of the counties in Colorado.
- ◼ More Indian people live in urban areas than live on the reservations.
- ◼ People of many Indian nations live in Colorado today.
- ◼ The Indian population in Colorado is increasing.
- ◼ Not all Indian people living in Colorado are full-blood Indians.

You know that the Southern Ute and Ute Mountain Ute people were forced to live on two small reservations in the southwestern part of the state. That was decided by treaties with the United States government. But why are so many Indian people living in urban areas?

The Six Colorado Counties with the Fewest Indian People in 2000

1. San Juan   4
2. Sedgwick   4
3. Mineral   7
4. Hinsdale   12
5. Jackson   12
6. Cheyenne   17

There is more than one reason that some Indian people now live off reservations.

During World War II, which was fought in Europe, Asia, and Africa, many American Indians served the United States as soldiers or warriors in these parts of the world. When the war was over, Indian soldiers were used to travel and life far from their reservations. Some decided that they could get good jobs and make better lives for their families in the cities. Many had learned new skills in the army that they wanted to use. They liked the many different opportunities for work and fun that they found in the city. If they were successful in the city, they usually stayed. They found jobs and made homes. Sometimes their friends and family joined them.

In the 1950s the government decided that it would be better for Indian people to live off of their reservations. They should learn to be like other Americans in the cities! The government believed that if Indian people lived away from their reservations, they would forget their Indian ways. Schools were started for Indian people to learn special skills and they were paid to move to cities. This was called "**relocation**." After they learned these new skills, they were supposed to be find jobs and make their homes in the city. Many had to promise not to return to their reservations to live. Before this policy ended, about half of the Indians in the United States were living in cities, not on reservations.

Although many Indian people were happy and successful in the city, others had a hard time. They didn't understand the ways of city living. They missed their families and communities. Some didn't speak English well. The jobs they were trained for didn't pay enough **wages** to take good care of their families. They didn't know how to find health care. Schools and transportation were confusing. They missed their ceremonies, celebrations, and Indian ways. They thought life in the city was lonely and frightening. Some decided to return to their reservations. But many others were more successful and stayed in the city.

Soon there were Indian organizations like the Denver Indian Center to help people live in the city. The center was a place to go to find other Indian people and to get help if they needed it. It was also a place to meet other Indian people and celebrate their Indian cultures.

When Indian families that lived in cities or on reservations had troubles that made it hard to care for their children, families who were not Indian adopted these Indian children. They were taken away from their families and communities and soon they forgot their Indian cultures. This made tribes weaker. Between 1969 and 1974, many Indian children were taken from their homes and adopted by non-Indian people.

Finally, a law was passed in 1978 to protect Indian children and tribes. It is called the American Indian Child Welfare Act. This law protects Indian children and cultures. This law says that Indian children must stay with their families or with other tribal people. Still, there are some Indian children who live in non-Indian families off of their reservations and homelands. Many of these children don't know very much about their Indian lifeways and cultures.

The government also started schools for Indian children that were both on and off reservations. Children were sent to schools in nearby cities or far from home. These children got used to speaking English and living away from their families and communities. Soon some of them were no longer comfortable in their Indian homes and did not want to return to their reservations to live. They wanted to stay in the city.

Indian Students in Denver Public Schools

Children from 65 Indian nations go to Denver Public Schools.

When Indian people who stayed in the cities began to meet many Indian people from different tribes other changes began to happen. Indian men and women would sometimes marry someone from another tribe or someone who wasn't Indian. If a Lakota woman married a Navajo man, their children would be part Lakota and part Navajo or Lakota/Navajo.

Events became **Pan-Indian** events. Pan-Indian means Indian, but not connected to just one tribe. For example, powwows that are held at the Denver Indian Center are Pan-Indian. Indian people from many tribes go to powwows to dance and drum. These are Pan-Indian powwows. There are foods that really aren't traditional but they are modern and Pan-Indian. Indian tacos are a favorite, modern Pan-Indian food.

You can see that there are many reasons that so many Indian people live in Colorado cities and towns. Some are closer to their Indian cultures than others. But, the number of Indian people in Colorado continues to grow in the urban areas and on the reservations.

Katrina Her Many Horses: Her Story

Hello. My name is Katrina Ann Her Many Horses. I am a member of the Cheyenne/Arapaho tribes of Oklahoma. The reservation is in Oklahoma, but my family lives in Denver. My last name comes from the Lakota side of my family. When I am home with my family or my relatives, everyone calls me "Trina." I go to school in Denver and I am in the third grade. My school friends and the teachers call me "Katrina".

I want to tell you about my family. It is like many other families in Denver. But, our family is Native American, so we are different in some ways too.

I really like my school. My favorite books are written by Dr. Seuss. I love to read books about other Native people too. My mom helps me with my homework every night. Her name is Terra. She is a nurse, but she doesn't work at night so she can be home with my brother, my sister, and me. My brother, Elias, is six years old and is in the first grade. My little sister Star is just three years old.

Let me tell you about the other people in my family who live with us. I have a big family, so someone is always home to play with. My family lives with my mother's parents. My grandmother is Meskwaki which is a tribe from Iowa My grandfather is from Taos Pueblo in New Mexico. My aunt and her family live with us too. My Aunt Aspen and Uncle Jarred have two children. My cousin Jordan is 8 years old and his sister is Jerra who is six years old.

I am lucky to have a big family. My grandmother lets me help her cook. I always get to choose what kind of cake I want for my birthday. Sometimes we try recipes from my new cookbook for kids. I help my grandfather work in the backyard too.

On birthdays and holidays our house and big backyard are filled with aunts, uncles, cousins, and friends. My birthday is very close to the Fourth of July, so we have a big barbecue and birthday party at our house. There are lots of kids and we play games, eat birthday cake and ice cream, and have fireworks too!

If you came to my house, Bitsy would bark at you. Bitsy is our little brown dog. She always barks at people who come to visit. Bitsy must think she is a great big dog! She likes to beg for doggie treats!

In our living room, there are two big pictures over the fireplace. They are pictures of my cousin and me dressed in our powwow outfits. I am a Fancy Shawl dancer. My mother is a Traditional dancer too. She makes our powwow regalia. When she was a girl, she carefully watched her parents beading until she learned how to bead. It takes her about two months to do the beading for one of our powwow outfits. My grandmother and grandfather do beadwork too. My mother says that braiding my hair is just as hard as beading my outfit! I know she's just joking . I want to learn how to do beadwork like my mother and grandmother. I have started beading my own little purse.

When winter is almost over and spring seems almost here, we start to get ready for the Denver March Pow*Wow. We go to small powwows in the winter, but the March Pow*Wow is special. Before I was 8 years old, I danced with the Tiny Tots. Now that I am older, I can dance in the Girls Junior Fancy Shawl contest. Elias and Star will still dance with the Tiny Tots.

My mother works hard to make my beautiful outfit. I am proud to dance to honor my mother, my family, and my culture. This year, my uncle, who is Cheyenne, will be one of the Master of Ceremonies and my grandpa, who is Lakota, will be the arena director. I like to visit with all of our friends and relatives at the Pow*Wow! My relatives always say that I have grown taller each year.

Tiny Tots are learning to dance so they don't have prizes. But this year I will dance in the Junior Girls Fancy Shawl contest, and maybe I will win a prize. I am excited about that. And, last of all, my mom lets me eat an Indian Taco every single day of the powwow. I like pizza and spaghetti too, but Indian Tacos are my very favorite food.

The Denver March Pow*Wow isn't the only powwow we go to. In the summer we dance at other large powwows in other parts of the country. This is called going on the powwow trail. These powwows are often outdoors. Some families camp outside in tents, trailers, or tipis. Others stay in motels. We usually stay in a motel. Our family likes to dance and we all support each other. We like to visit with old and new friends on the powwow trail. This is one way we celebrate our Native cultures.

There are so many ways that my family is like most families. But, just like your family is special, our Indian family is special too. I am very proud to be a member of the Cheyenne/Arapaho Nation.

Ceriss Blackwood: Her Story

My name is Ceriss Blackwood and I work with the Indian Education Project in Denver Public Schools. Sometimes the Indian children who go to our large city schools feel alone because there aren't a lot of Indian kids in their school. These kids are from many tribes and go to many different schools in Denver. My job is to help the Indian kids with their school work if they need help, but more importantly, I help them get to know the other Indian kids and learn about American Indian cultures. We work together and have fun too! I also work along with the parents of the Indian kids to help them be successful in school.

My early childhood was filled with problems, challenges, and lots of struggles. Later, as a teenager, my Southern Ute family and Indian culture helped me to succeed and to be strong. Now, it is important to me to give my knowledge and skills back to the Indian community. Let me tell you my story.

Right after I was born, I went to live with my grandmother. She is a strong woman who loved and took care of me. As I grew up, she always supported and encouraged me. But when I was seven years old, I went to live with my father. This change was the beginning of very hard years for me. My father had some troubles and we moved many times. We lived in all kinds of places in many communities. Because we moved so much, I went to as many as five different schools. As a new kid in so many schools, it was hard for me to learn. Every school and every teacher was different. It wasn't easy to make friends when we moved so much. Lots of time the other children would bully and tease me.

When I should have been going to school for 8th grade to 10th grade, my father took me out of school and I went to work instead. The places where I worked were bad for me. The people were not kind, the work was too hard, and sometimes I got hurt. I quickly learned that I wanted a different life and that I needed a good education to have the kind of life I wanted.

Next, I went to live with my foster mother, Geraldine Rael, who lived on the Southern Ute Reservation in Ignacio. This is the person that I now call "Mom." She is the woman who gave me a good home and a strong family that took care of me in many ways. The people in this family are enrolled as members of the Southern Ute Nation and follow traditional Ute ways. Because my Mom and grandfather also have family roots at Picuris Pueblo, some of their traditions are from there too.

In Ignacio, my life was safe and stable. My Mom made sure I ate good food, went to school, did my homework, and was part of her family. I lived in a nice home in a beautiful environment, and I was accepted! We lived like a normal Ute family. At dinner, we made a spirit plate and said the right prayers. My Grandfather Joe led our sweat lodges and taught me the things I needed to know. My mom worked for the tribe. Like a lot of other American families, we often ate meals to go because of my Mom's busy schedule. Soon, I was earning good grades and making wonderful friends. I was really home!

After I graduated from high school. I chose to go to college. I graduated from Colorado State University with a bachelor's degree and I am planning to continue to go to school to earn a master's degree. In the future, I want to return to the Ute Reservation to live with my family and work with the tribe. As a educated Indian woman, I have much to share and to give. Southern Ute is my my home, and my family. This is where I am safe and where I belong.

More Books to Read

Hobbs, Will. *Beardream*. New York, NY: Atheneum, 1997.

Hoyt-Goldsmith, Diane. *Pueblo Story Teller*. New York, NY: Holiday House, 1991.

Raczek, Linda T. *The Night the Grandfathers Danced*. Flagstaff, AZ: Northland, 1995.

Rendon, Marcie R. *Powwow Summer*. Minneapolis, MN: Carolrhoda, 1996.

Places to Go

Denver Indian Center
4407 Morrison Road
Denver, CO 80219-2464
(303) 936-2688

Websites to Visit

Denver March Pow*Wow: www.denvermarchpowwow.org

Southern Ute Drum (newspaper): www.southern-ute.nsn.us/drum/

Things to Do

Do you know someone who is Indian?
Is there someone in your community who is Indian? Ask them to talk to you about their family Make a list of the questions you want to ask them.

Reading about Indians who don't live in Coloado
Read books about American Indian children. A librarian can help you find many books about families and children from different tribes in the United States. Look for books written by Indian people too.

Indian foods
Make a list of foods that are traditional Indian foods. Some foods like corn, squash, and beans are foods that Europeans didn't have before Columbus. You will need to do some research!

Cook some Indian Food!

Fry Bread
4 1/2 cups all-purpose flour
1 tablespoon baking powder
2 tablespoons non-fat dry milk powder
1 teaspoon salt

1 1/2 cups warm water

1 cup vegetable oil for frying

Combine flour, baking powder, dry milk powder, and salt. Gradually add warm water and mix with dry ingredients to form a soft firm ball. Knead in bowl or on a lightly floured surface until smooth - about 10 minutes.

Separate dough in 8-10 small pieces and pat circles of dough about 3/8 inches thick. Put a hole into the center.

Slip dough rounds into hot fat and fry, turning once, about 2 minutes on each side, until puffy and brown. Drain on a paper towel or in a paper bag. This is great to do in a heavy skillet over an open fire. Use a long pointed stick to poke into the hole in the bread to turn it or take it out of the fire.

To make Indian Tacos, put a combination of beans and browned hamburger, lettuce, tomato, onion, and cheese on top of the fry bread. Add salsa, if you like. Or put honey or Wojapi on your fry bread.

Traditional Wojapi

1 cup fruit (blueberries, cherries, strawberries, chokecherries)

1 cup water

Sugar to taste

Flour as needed.

Heat fruit and water to boiling. Add sugar to taste. Gradually blend in some flour a little at a time until it is thick enough. Stir it all the time. Eat as a pudding. Delicious on fry bread.

Today's Wojapi

Canned blueberry/raspberry/strawberry pie filling. Eat as a pudding. Delicious on fry bread too.

Definitions

Census	a count of the people living in the United States that is taken every ten years
Pan-Indian	Indians in general, not a specific tribe
Relocation	to move to another place or location
Rural	where a few people live far apart in a large area like the country
Urban	where many people live close together in an area like a city
Wages	payment for work done

Forward to Tomorrow

After the terrible times, many battles, treaties, speeches, and government policies made many people think that Indians would soon become extinct. After all, they had heard government people say things like "The only good Indian is a dead Indian" Colorado newspapers had told their readers that "The Utes Must Go!"

Many people thought that Indian people and their values, beliefs, and traditions would be lost forever. Government policies would certainly make Indian people forget their languages and their ways of life! They believed that Indians would become a part of the history of the United States, not be a part of the future.

Like all people and cultures, Indians in Colorado changed over time. But, they are not extinct. Their population is growing. They are thriving. Today, Indian people live, work, and raise families in Colorado cities and on Colorado reservations. They don't live in tipis or wickiups. They don't hunt and gather all of their food for their families. They don't wear clothes made of animal skins, feathers, and woven grasses. They live in today's world and plan for a good future.

Grace, Katrina, and Eddie are proud to be citizens of their tribes and the United States of America. Their family and Indian values shape who they are and who they will be in the future.

Goals For The Future

There are important goals that guide many Indian tribes and families. Goals are something you want to happen and you work to achieve. They tell about what people want for themselves and their families. Goals help people make good decisions for their lives. These goals for Indian families and tribes are linked together. They are not separate.

To reach big, important goals takes time, work, and courage. People, families, groups, organizations, and governments often take years and years to reach their goals. Sometimes they take huge, successful steps forward and other times they take little, baby steps. To reach a goal, it is important to keep working and reaching until the goals are met.

Important Goals For Indian Tribes and Families

1 Getting Ready for the Future

All families and cultures guide their children as they grow to be adults. They help them get ready for the future. In the past, Indian children learned how to survive by watching and helping their parents, grandparents, and other people. They learned values and traditions by listening to stories and by experience.

Today our world is a global world. This world is much bigger than families, tribes, towns or cities. We live in a global community and are linked to people in all countries. New technology, like the

Internet, makes us global neighbors. In this global world, kids must learn to read, write, and understand math and science. They must learn how to communicate with others who have different values and traditions. Also, they must know how make good decisions and solve problems. It is important to understand and work with other people. Education prepares young people for a new future with possibilities we don't even know about yet!

Reaching For The Goal

On the Southern Ute Reservation, the people decided that a school for Ute children would be the best way to get their kids ready for a global world. They believed that their children would be more successful in schools that understood the importance of their history, language, and culture. Ute parents and the community wanted a school that was a Ute school. They wanted their children to learn reading, writing, math, social studies, science, music and art in a school that taught them in the ways they learned best and with Ute teachers. Most of all, they wanted them to be strong and capable as members of the Southern Ute Nation and as American and global citizens.

After much thought, they decided that their school would be a Montesorri school. Montesorri schools teach in special ways that are much like the traditional ways that Ute children learned long ago. The goals of the Montesorri school are much the same as public schools, but the ways the students reach these goals are different. There are many Montesorri schools all over the world and the Ute people believed that these ways of learning would be good for their children. The name of the new Southern Ute school is Pinunuuchi P'gani.

The Ute people were right! The school is successful and their children are learning well. Their teachers, parents, relatives, and community members made a good decision for their children and their futures.

2 Keeping our Cultures and Traditions

When you think about American Indian cultures and traditions, remember that, like all families, Indian families are not alike. Some live on reservations with their family living close around them. Indian people who live on reservations have leaders, laws, and traditions that are part of family, school, and every day community life. It is easy for kids who live on their reservations to learn their culture.

Other Indian families live in towns and cities. Their relatives could be close by or far away. Urban families may have their roots in different tribes with different traditions. Often families that don't live on reservations, go "home" to the reservations for special family events, like weddings. Or they may return to the reservation for dances like the Bear Dance, or ceremonies like the Sun Dance. In many ways, it is harder for children to learn their culture in the city.

On the reservations, people don't want their languages to disappear. So they teach their language in schools and homes. They have elders come to the school to teach their language and tell stories about their traditions. In the city, it is harder to keep Indian languages alive. There are many Indian languages from different tribes in most urban communities. It isn't possible to teach so many languages in the schools. Often, children in city schools learn their language from their parents or the elders in the family who

Days of the week in the Ute Language

- Sunday   saatavai
- Monday   kwasutavai
- Tuesday   waikutugwarikyetu
- Wednesday peikutugwarikyetu
- Thursday   wchukutugwarikyetu
- Friday   suwasaavaru
- Saturday   saavaru

SOURCE: Southern Ute Website - Academy newsletter

still speak the languages they learned when they were children. And, sometimes they don't learn them at all.

Reaching For The Goal

There are some Indian traditions that are much the same from tribe to tribe, and on reservations and in urban areas. Perhaps the most important is the **extended family**. Families often include grandparents, aunts, uncles, and cousins who live in the same house or close by. Children may live with grandparents or aunts and uncles, especially when their own family needs some help. When families live far from their extended family, groups or organizations like the Denver Indian Center become their extended family. They are ready to help families who need support.

Another important Indian value is respect for elders. Indian people respect the wisdom of older people. They know that their elders have had many experiences in their lives and have much knowledge to share and teach. To show their respect, they often call elders in the community "Grandmother" or "Grandfather." Grandparents are important family members and they help take care of the children. Indian elders are cared for by the family members. But, sometimes that isn't possible. Recently many tribes have built special homes for elderly Indian people whose families cannot take care of them.

A Giveaway at the Powwow

Grace's cousin John is graduating from college this year. He is going to be a computer programmer. He learned how to use the computer and the Internet in the third grade. He always did a lot of his school work on the computer. He likes to play computer games too.

John is the first person in his family to graduate from college. His family has worked hard to help him. He has started a great new job as a computer programmer. Now, he earns good wages by doing something that he has always liked to do. John also wants to help his sister go to college to learn to be a teacher.

For almost a year, Grace's family has been gathering special things for a giveaway to honor John's hard work and achievement. They store things for the giveaway in Grace's Aunt Rose's basement. With the whole family helping out, the pile of gifts gets bigger every week.

They have filled about ten big plastic baskets filled with food and fruit, towels, bowls and dishes, handmade pillows decorated with Indian designs, and other household things. Gifts of tobacco and sweetgrass are gifts that will be used in ceremonies. Star quilts are carefully folded in big plastic bags and stacked on shelves. These quilts are handmade by John's mother, grandmother, aunts, and cousins. Star quilts are beautiful and are given to show honor and appreciation. **Pendleton blankets** with Indian designs are stored on the shelves too. Grace and John's Aunt Linda also made five pretty shawls for dancing. For the singers and drummers, they have gifts of soda pop and water.

On the day of the powwow, the family loads their van with the gifts and brings them into the powwow arena. Grace is excited about the giveaway. She helps carry the gifts and arrange them in the arena. The drums begin the giveaway with a traditional honor song. As the family dances around the arena, people join them in honor of John's graduation. John's whole family is dancing. Everyone in the community is proud of John. Grace wants to go to college too and she thinks about how hard John worked to reach his goal.

After the honor song, the family stands in a line beside the gifts at one end of the arena. They stand tall and proud. John's grandfather talks for the family. He talks about the family's pride in his grandson's achievement and how his hard work honors his family and tribe.

Then, one by one, the family calls people to the arena to receive their gifts. After they accept their gifts, they walk down the line of family members to congratulate and thank them. They shake the hand of each person in the family. Sometimes this takes a really long time!

There are some gifts left so, in the Indian way, John's family gives them to the elders and moms in the arena. Finally, a big bag of candy is scattered on the floor for all the tiny tots. The little children come running to get pieces of candy. This giveaway honors John, his family and community, and their Indian values.

Something to Think About

If you could give a **star quilt** to an American Indian to honor his/her achievement, who would you choose? Why?

Indians are generous people. The giveaway at the pow-wow is one of many ways Indian people show their generosity. A giveaway is when a family gathers many gifts of blankets, quilts, and food as gifts. In the past, they would give horses too. These gifts are given to honor a person or event. A giveaway at a pow-wow might honor a birthday or graduation, or an achievement like serving as a soldier, or being chosen as a head dancer at a powwow.

3 Taking Charge of Our Lives

In the past, Indian people had leaders and ways of governing their lives. Fathers,

The Future for All of Us

"Whenever the white man treats an Indian as they treat each other, then we will have no more wars. We shall all be alike—brothers of one father and one mother, with one sky above us and one country around us, and one government for all." (Chief Joseph - 1879)

SOURCE: Vanderwerth, W. C. (comp). Indian Oratory: Famous Speeches by Noted Indian Chieftains (6th ed.). Norman, OK: University of Oklahoma, 1989. pp. 283-284.

mothers, and grandparents made rules and decisions for their families. Tribal leaders would make decisions for their tribes. There were Peace Chiefs who managed hunts and helped to settle arguments. Also, there were War Chiefs for times of war.

Then, for a long time, the United States government made decisions for Indian people. Indians often called the president of the United States the "Great White Father." This made Indian people feel like children, not adults. It is very important to them to **govern** themselves and not be treated like children.

Today, there are laws that say that tribes can manage their own lives and make rules for their own people. This makes Indian people citizens of their tribe, their city, their state, and the United States of America. Tribal leaders in Colorado are called Chairmen (not Chiefs). **Tribal councils** make business and other decisions for the tribe. The tribes have their own police officers. The people elect chairman and council members. Today, women can be elected to be tribal leaders too.

Water for the Ute Mountain Utes

There is an old story that a Ute Chief once stood in the San Juan Mountains of Colorado and said, "From where I stand, all the land this water touches belongs to the Ute people."

Utes have fought to save their right to the water that they needed to survive. Chief Jack House, the last traditional chief, knew how important the water was to his people. He used his power as chief to fight to bring water back to the Ute people.

Finally, the Utes won those rights in a new law. It was called the Colorado Ute Indian Water Rights Settlement Act of 1988. Now, Life-giving water flows onto Ute land.

SOURCE: Adapted from the Ute Mountain Ute website.

Reaching For the Goal

In Colorado, the Colorado Commission on Indian Affairs is a part of the Lieutenant Governor's office. The Commission works to help the state government and the governments of the two Indian reservations work together for Indian people. There are eleven members of the Commission. Two members are the Southern Ute Reservation and two members are from the Ute Mountain Ute Reservation. Two other members are chosen by the Commission. The other members are non-Indian leaders of the Colorado government. Today the governments of the Southern Ute and the Ute Mountain Ute work with the government of Colorado to find answers to problems and to make decisions for the future.

4 Building Strong Families and Communities

Strong communities protect and support their families. They help children be safe, healthy, and grow strong and ready for the future. Communities support families in many ways.

Ernest D. House, Jr. (Ute Mountain Ute): An Indian Leader

Ernest House is a young, proud leader in the Ute Mountain Tribe of Colorado. He was also the Executive Secretary for the Colorado Commission of Indian Affairs.

Ernest is a graduate of the Montezuma-Cortez High School. He studied government at a college in Denver. His culture and the education that he has earned made him a strong leader in his tribe and in Colorado.

Members of his family have been Ute Mountain Ute leaders for a long time. His father is Ernest House, Sr. who has been a leader and worked for the tribe for about forty years. He is also the great-grandson of Chief Jack House who was the last Traditional Chief of the Ute Mountain Ute Tribe. Chief Jack House died in 1971. His picture is on the **dome** or ceiling of the Colorado State Capitol along with the picture of Buckskin Charlie, the last traditional chief of the Southern Utes.

In the past, people lived in extended family communities to survive. Men did the hunting and protected the people. Women took care of children, crops, and the home. Boys learned the work of men and girls learned the work of women. Everyone had a job to do and families thrived.

Today life has changed on Indian reservations. Men and women have different kind of jobs. They work for wages or money. Their wages buy food, clothing, and shelter. Wages pay for doctors, dentists, eye glasses, and medicine. When people have jobs, they pay taxes to their governments. This tax money builds community schools, day care for children, hospitals, libraries, recreation centers, and roads. Taxes also pay for police officers, fire fighters, garbage collection, and other things that make communities safe.

If jobs are not available or people don't have the skills to find jobs, their families have a hard time. They may not have enough money for a safe home, healthy food, warm clothes, good schools or health care. If they don't have jobs, they can't pay taxes. Then communities won't have the services that people need to be safe. Without money, the people and communities have to live without the things they need to be strong and healthy.

Reaching For the Goal

The Southern Utes and the Ute Mountain reservations are on lands where water was scarce and farming was difficult. In the past, there were few businesses that had jobs for the people. It was hard for people to find work. They had to find ways to create jobs for people so their families and communities could **thrive**.

The Southern Utes discovered natural gas on the reservation. Natural gas is a very valuable resource that is found underground. It is used for heating homes and kitchen stoves. Now, because natural gas is on their land, the Southern Utes are a **wealthy** tribe. They have built beautiful offices for their government and a school for their children. Each tribal member is given a part of the money made by the tribe from their natural gas.

Another part of this money is used for community services for all the people. The rest of this money is saved and used to make more money for the tribe in the future. If their children want to go to college, the tribe will pay for all of their expenses. The Southern Utes believe that this is a good way to prepare for a strong future. They know that the natural gas won't last forever. The tribe now has more jobs than any other business in the surrounding county.

Chief Ernest House Sr. worked to bring water to the The Ute Mountain Utes Reservation. In the past, water for drinking, cooking, and bathing had to be brought to families by truck from Cortez to Towaoc. There was no water for growing crops or raising animals. In 1988 a law was passed which allowed water to come to the reservation. With water, the people can farm and ranch and take care of their families.

Also, they are developing other businesses that create jobs for the people. They have built a large hotel and gambling **casino**. The hotel and casino have many jobs for the people. When tourists come to the casino, they want a place to stay, food to eat, and gas for their cars. This creates even more jobs. The tribe has also built a new building for their government. These businesses are good for the community.

The Ute Mountain Utes also have a natural resource that provides jobs. The Ute Mountain Tribal Park is a beautiful park that has many Ancient Puebloan sites. Visitors may not enter the park without a Ute guide. The Ute guides help protect these ancient sites. There is a visitor center, museum, and camp grounds in the park. The park creates many jobs for their people. Hundreds of tourists visit the beautiful park to see the ruins and camp on these ancient lands.

In the urban areas, some Indian people may have trouble finding jobs or don't have their extended family to help them when they need it. There are Indian organizations in the cities that are like extended families and can help them in many ways. Some organizations train people for jobs, keep kids out of trouble, supply food, find good homes, and provide health care and legal services. Some just bring Indian people together to be with other Indian people and have fun.

The Denver Indian Center is one of many organizations that support Indian people in the city. The center is led by a board of urban Indian people from many tribes. They offer many programs for Indian youth, adults, elders, and veterans too. The center helps people find jobs: keeps a food bank for people who don't have work and need food; is making plans for for a Montesorri pre-school program; supports elders in staying safe and healthy; organizes clubs and sport teams for teens; and hosts lots of social events like powwows for urban Indians to come together to dance and celebrate their traditions.

> **Denver Indian Center Mission Statement:** To empower our youth, families and community through self-determination, cultural identity and education.

Jay Grimm (Navajo): An Indian Leader

Jay Grimm is the Director of the Denver Indian Center. Often when people think of Indian leaders, they remember the wise, old chiefs of the past who taught, cared for, and led their people. Jay is a young man with a college degree, lots of energy, and a vision of a strong, exciting, **sustainable** future for Native urban people. He is an Indian leader of the present and the future who is guided by the wisdom and values of the past.

Jay is a member of the Navajo Nation. His mother is Navajo but his father is not. He was born in Denver and as a child, he lived in Aurora, a suburb of Denver. He went to public schools and was a happy, active "All

American" kid. Jay liked school and, like all kids, he loved riding his bike and hanging out with his friends. He was the class comedian and just a regular guy.

Tall and athletic, he liked all sports. He also loved music and played the piano and guitar in elementary school. Then in high school he played football, basketball, and Lacrosse and was also in the marching band and the jazz band.

But, Jay spent his summers in a different way than his neighborhood pals. Every summer he would spend time with his grandparents on the Navajo reservation. Living with his grandparents helped him appreciate and respect his roots. Being a part of everyday Navajo life helped him learn the Navajo language and understand his mother's Indian values. The land and lifeways of the **Diné** became a part of who he is now.

After earning a college degree, his first job was with an Indian organization in Washington D.C. that worked to make sure the members of the United States Congress knew what tribal and urban Indian people needed. He learned about the serious problems of many Indian people in all parts of the country. This was a very important job for a young man and it shaped his future. It taught him the skills needed to work with large organizations and the government. Recently, an urban **foundation** recognized his skills and gave him a large sum of money to continue his study of leadership.

Today, Jay lives in Denver with his wife, two daughters and one dog. Ellison is three years old and Anaba is one year old. Cleo, the dog, is a retired racing greyhound who now is a "couch potato" instead of a racer. Being a good husband and father are very important goals for Jay.

Another goal is to achieve his vision for the Denver Indian Center. Jay wants to develop an urban Indian center that will be the center of Denver's Indian community. This center would have a pre-school, health clinic, art gallery, gift shop, restaurant, meeting rooms, library, computer labs, small businesses, food banks, employment assistance, and anything else that is needed by the community to be strong, vital, and independent. This center would be the hub of the Indian community. With Jay's energy, experience, skills, and leadership, it could happen!

Sometimes other people in the city become like an extended family. In Denver schools, there is a new group of teenage girls who meet together with strong women mentors. The mentors are like aunts in an Indian family. They are friends, teachers, and coaches to the girls. They usually meet together during the week, but sometimes they do special things on the weekends too. The girls talk with their mentors and decide what things they would like to do or learn about.

This year, they have learned how to use a sewing machine and made their dresses to wear at a traditional **sweat lodge**. They have learned some ways to help them make good decisions for their lives. They visited a beauty school to explore a career that interested some of the girls. They got a manicure at the school too! Now, they are planning to have lunch in several restaurants that serve food that is new to them. They are also learning about nutrition and how to cook and eat healthy foods. With the help of their mentors, they are preparing for a good future.

Dr. Sara Jumping Eagle (Oglala Lakota): An Indian Leader

Sara Jumping Eagle was one of the mentors that worked with these girls. Dr. Jumping Eagle has two names. Her Lakota name, Red Shell Woman, was given to her by a Medicine Man. It is the name of one of her ancestors. Sara had a dream from the time she was ten years old. She was living with her grandmother in California when her grandmother was training to become a nurse. Sara dreamed of becoming a doctor. When she was eleven, she moved back to the reservation with her grandparents and her brother and sister.

Sara loved school on the reservation and she made many friends. History and biology were her favorite subjects. In seventh grade she began to go to a special program in the summer. This program is called Indians Into Medicine. For six weeks each summer when she was in junior and senior high school, she lived on the campus of the University of North Dakota and studied the subjects that would help her to be a doctor someday. In the program, she also learned about the roles of doctors by watching them as they did their work. When she graduated from the University of North Dakota, she was accepted into medical school at Stanford University. She kept working hard to achieve her dream.

As a doctor, Sara began her work at Children's Hospital in Denver and she also worked at Denver Indian Health and Family Services. She met with patients and she also did research at the University of Colorado that will lead to new discoveries in medicine.

Sara is married to Chase Iron Eyes (Standing Rock Sioux). Her husband studied to become a lawyer at the University of Denver. Now, in North Dakota, their family is a strong part of the community, and with their professional training and skills, they continue to give much to Indian people.

These four goals for American Indian people are very large goals. They are goals that people work toward for a lifetime. They are goals for one person, for one family, for one community, for one Indian nation, and for all people. Sometimes big steps are made and sometimes little steps are taken. Sometimes people take a step that is backward, not forward, and have to change to get back on the right road. These powerful goals are a way to a good future for Indian people and their cultures. Indian people would say that the goals are the "red road" or the right road for Indian people.

More Books to Read

Ortiz, Simon. *The People Shall Continue.* San Francisco, CA: Children's Book Press, 1988.

Websites to Visit

Colorado Commission on Indian Affairs
http://www.colorado.gov/ltgovernor/initiatives/indianaffairs.html

Denver Indian Center http://www.denverindiancenter.org

Southern Ute http://www.southern-ute.nsn.us/

Ute Mountain Ute http://www.utemountainute.com

Radio

Listen to the Southern Ute radio station: http://www.ksut.org/

Things to Do

Star Quilts and Blankets

Research one of the following:

- ■ * Star quilts
- ■ * Pendleton blankets (How are they connected to the American Indian College Fund?)

Goals

- ■ Make a list of four big goals for your life or your family.
- ■ Think of one thing you can do to reach for each goal.

The Southern Ute Montesorri Academy

Read about the Southern Ute school on their website - click on Montesorri: http://www.southern-ute.nsn.us/

The Meaning of Survival

Read the book, *We Shall Continue,* by Simon Ortiz. What is the lesson in this book? Do you agree with the author?

Definitions

Casino	a building used for gambling
Diné	the traditional name of the Navajo people
Dome	a rounded ceiling
Extended family	includes parents, grandparents, aunts, uncles, cousins, and sometimes friends

Foundation	an organization that gives money for research or study
Govern	to control, direct, or rule
Mentor	a coach or guide
Pendleton blankets	wool blankets originally made for trade with the Indians
Sustainable	to maintain at the same level
Star quilt	handmade quilt with a large star in the center and given to honor others
Sweat Lodge	a sacred ceremony that is held to clean a person's body and spirit
Thrive	to grow and move closer to goals
Tribal Council	a small group of people elected to make rules for the tribe
Wealthy	having plenty of money

Chapter 10

Dancing with Grace

Grace stood quietly, waiting for the first drum beat. So far, she had danced in every Grand Entry and in every Junior Girl's Jingle Dress contest. Now she was ready to dance in the very last Jingle Dress Contest for this year. The judges, holding their score sheets, were standing around the arena. They will watch the girls carefully as they dance. The judges will judge each dancer on her regalia, if she knows the song so she can can stop exactly on the last beat, and her conduct or her demeanor. The dancers should dance with dignity and respect for themselves, other dancers, and their culture. They should dance with grace and beauty.

For just a minute, Grace was a little nervous. Then the song began. She knew that she wasn't dancing to win a contest, she was dancing because she was Indian and it was good to dance. She danced to honor her community. She danced in respect for her family who made her beautiful dance regalia and supported her. Her jingles made a joyful sound and the drums sounded like her heartbeat. She danced with happiness and stopped exactly on the last beat of the drum!

When the dance ended, the girls made a line in front of the judges so that they could make certain that they had the the right numbers for the right girls on their score sheets. Then they went to sit with their families and wait for the announcement of the dance contest winners.

This was a good powwow for Grace. She had visited with many friends and with her family members who didn't live in Denver. She ate at least three Indian tacos. She used her allowance money to buy a braid of sweetgrass and a small dream catcher. Now, her heart skipped a little beat as she heard the Master of Ceremonies begin to announce the winners of the dance contests. He started with the youngest dancers. Grace sat quietly with her parents and waited.

Then he began to announce the winners of the Junior Girls Jingle Dress Contest. First, the third place winner, then the second place winner, then the first place winner. Grace heard her name called. She ran forward to shake the hands of the judges and then waited to shake the hands of all of the dance contest winners. She had won $100 and a beautiful jacket. Grace danced gracefully with respect for herself and others. She is going to save her prize money to go college. This is another way to honor her family and her culture!

Glossary

Acre	an acre is 4840 square yards with 640 acres in a square mile
Adobe	a brick or building material of sun-dried earth and straw
Agency	an official United States government office on Indian reservations
Allotment	a 160 acre piece of land given to someone to farm
Ancestor	a family member that lived a long time ago
Ancient Puebloans	the more accurate name that has replaced "Anasazi", the people of Mesa Verde who were the ancestors of today's Pueblo people
Ancient	old or from a long time ago
Annuities	the food, tools, and other goods promised to the Indians in the treaties
Apishapa	ancient people who lived in Southeastern Colorado
Archaeologists	scientists who study of any prehistoric culture by digging and studying the artifacts that they find
Arena	a flat, round enclosed area where the dancers dance
Artifact	any object used or made by a human being
Assembled	gathered together
Bale	a package held together by wire or rope
Band	a group of people who live and work together
Banned	not allowed
Basin	shaped like a bowl
Casino	a building used for gambling
Celebration	the ceremonies or festivities held to observe a day or commemorate an event, a person, or a culture
Census	a count of the people living in the United States that is taken every ten years
Claim	to say something belongs to you
Climate	the type of weather found in an area
Cholera	a disease that causes severe diarrhea and often death
Coliseum	a large building built for public event

Continental Divide	an imaginary line across the tops of the mountains; rivers on the west flow to the west and rivers on the east flow to the east.
Creator	the name given to the God that people worshipped
Culture Areas	the name scientists gave to environments that were much alike
Demeanor	a person's behavior
Descendants	the members of the family that were born after them; their children, grandchildren, great-grandchildren and so on.
Desert Culture	the people who lived west of the plains in the mountains, foothills, and plateau areas around the Colorado river as early as 7000 B. C.
Diné	the traditional name of the Navajo people
Dome	a rounded ceiling
Drought	a very long period where there is no rainfall for the crops
Elevation	how high or low the land is compared to sea level
Environment	the climate, landforms, and natural resources that surround us
Extended family	includes parents, grandparents, aunts, uncles, cousins, and sometimes friends
Extinct	no longer exists
fl.	the high point of a person's life or career when his/her dates of birth are unknown
Four Corners	the area around the place where New Mexico, Arizona, Utah, and Colorado meet
Generous	to give much
Govern	to control, direct, or rule
Incident	an action or situation that is likely to have a bad effect
Intruder	a person who enters without invitation, permission, or welcome
Landforms	the shape and features of the land - like mountains, plains, plateaus, basins, oceans, and rivers
Ledgerbook	a small book with lined pages that Indian people got from Americans and used to draw pictures that recorded events in their history

Lifeways	the ways people live - their homes, foods, clothing, families, arts and crafts, laws and leaders, trade, beliefs and values, and traditions
Lodge	a lodge can be a home, or it can mean a club of members who share beliefs and ceremonies that are alike
Mano	a stone that grinds corn on metate
Manifest Destiny	the belief in the 1840s that the United States should expand or spread across the continent, by force if necessary. This would be good for everybody, including the American Indians.
Massacre	the killing of a large number of defenseless people
Mentor	a coach or guide
Mesa	a raised area of land with a flat top and steep sides
Mesa Verde	a high plateau in southwestern Colorado that was the home of the Ancient Puebloans
Metate	a flat stone with high sides; a mano is used to grind corn and meat on a metate
Morache	a musical instrument made from a notched stick; its sound is like the growl of a bear
Motto	a short way of communicating the meaning of an idea
Mountain	a natural raised part of the earth larger than a hill.
Natural Resources	those things in nature that people use such as trees, plants, animals, soil, and water
Negotiate	to try to reach an agreement by discussion and compromise
Nomads	people who have no permanent home but move from place to place to gather food (plants, roots, berries) and hunt game (animals, birds, fish, insects)
Paleo-Indians	ancient Indians
Pan-Indian	Indians in general, not a specific tribe
Parfleche	an untanned animal skin folded to make a carrying case
Pendleton	blankets wool blankets originally made for trade with the Indians
Permanent	stays the same or in the same place
Pioneer	the first non-Indian people to settle in a territory
Plain	a big open area of flat land

Plateau	an area of high flat land surrounded by one or more mountains
Policy	a government plan of action
Powwow	an event where Indian people come together to be with friends, dance, feast, and trade
Precipitation	rain, snow, or any other kind of moisture that falls from the sky
Prehistoric	before history was written down
Regalia	the special clothing worn for powwow dancing
Relocation	to move to another place or location
Resign	to give up your job or position
Ritual	a special way of doing things
Rural	where a few people live far apart in a large area like the country
Sacred	something that is worthy of great honor and respect
Seasonal Round	when people follow the seasons to find food and come back to the same places each year
Sherds (also, shards)	pieces of ancient pottery
Sinew	an animal tendon that is used as a cord or thread
Society	a military society is like a club
Slaughter	to kill in large numbers
Spectators	people who watch an event
Star quilt	handmade quilt with a large star in the center that is often given to honor others
Starve	to suffer or die from not having enough food
Survive	to live and not die
Sustainability	to maintain at a certain level
Sweat Lodge	a sacred ceremony that is held to clean a person's body and spirit
Symbol	something that stands for something else
Thrive	to grow and move closer to goals
Treaty	a written agreement between two countries
Tribal Council	a small group of people elected to make rules for the tribe
Tipi	a home shaped like a cone which is made with logs and covered with hides

Traditions	ways of thinking, acting, celebrating, and believing that are handed down by word of mouth from one generation to another
Travois	a sled made of poles and hides that is pulled by a dog or horse
Urban	where many people live close together in an area like a city
Wages	payment for work done
Wealthy	having plenty of money
Wickiup	temporary camp shelters that were used before and shortly after the Ute obtained the horse

Indians in Colorado: A Bibliography

Resources for Children
Information Books:

Arnold, Caroline. *The Ancient Cliff Dwellers of Mesa Verde*. New York, NY: Clarion, 1992.

Ashabranner, Brent. *Morning Star, Black Sun*. New York, NY: Putnam, 1982.

Berman, Ruth. *American Bison*. Minneapolis, MN: Carolrhoda, 1992.

Bial, Raymond. *The Arapaho*. New York, NY: Benchmark, 2004.

Bial, Raymond. *The Cheyenne*. New York, NY: Benchmark, 2001.

Bonvillain, Nancy. *The Cheyennes: People of the Plains*. Brookfield, CT: Millbrook, 1996.

Brodsky, Beverly. *Buffalo*. New York, NY: Cavendish 2003.

Engler, Mary. *The Cheyenne: Hunter-Gathers of the Northern Plains*. Mankata, MN: Capstone, 2004.

Fisher, Leonard. E. *Anasazi*. New York, NY: Atheneum, 1997.

Flanagan, Alice K. *The Utes*. Danbury, CT: Children's Press. 1998.

Fowler, Loretta. *The Arapaho*. New York, NY: Chelsea, 1989.

Fradin, Dennis *The Cheyenne*. Danbury, CT: Children's Press,. 1994. (ages 4-8)

Freeman, Brian and Jodi Freeman. *The Old Ones*. Albuquerque, NM: The Think Shop, 1986.

Freedman, Russell. *Buffalo Hunt*. New York, NY: Holiday House, 1988.

Gardner, Mark L. *Bent's Old Fort*. Tucson, AZ: Southwest Parks and Monuments Association, 1998.

Gibson, Karen B. *The Arapaho: Hunters of the Plains*. Mankato, MN: Bridgestone, 2003.

Haluska, Vicki. *The Arapaho Indians*. New York, NY: Chelsea, 1993.

Hoig, Stan. *The Cheyenne*. New York, NY: Chelsea, 1989.

Hoig, Stan. *People of the Sacred arrows: The Southern Cheyenne Today*. New York, NY:Dutton, 1992.

Hoyt-Goldsmith, Diane. *Buffalo Days*. New York, NY: Holiday House, 1997.

Lassieur, Allison. *The Utes*. Mankato, MN: Bridgestone, 2002.

Marsh, Charles S. *People of the Shining Mountains*. Boulder, CO: Pruett, 1982.

Myers, Arthur. *The Cheyenne*. New York, NY: Franklin Watts, 1992.

Petersen, David. 1992. *Mesa Verde National Park*. Danbury, CT: Children's Press.

Remington, Gwen. *The Cheyenne*. San Diego, CA: Lucent, 2001.

Shuter, Jane. *Visiting the Past: Mesa Verde*. Chicago, IL: Heinemann Library, 2000.

Sita, Lisa. *Indians of the Great Plains: Traditions, History, Legends, and Life*. Milwaukee: WI: Gareth Stevens, 2000.

Sneve, Virginia Driving Hawk. *The Cheyennes*. New York, NY: Holiday House, 1996.

Sonneborn, Liz *The Cheyenne Indians*. New York, NY: Chelsea, 1994.

Swanson, Diane. *Buffalo Sunrise: The Story of a North American Giant*. San Francisco, CA: Sierra Club Books for Children, 1996.

Taylor, David. *The Bison and the Great Plains*. New York, NY: Crabtree, 1990.

Terry, Michael Bad Hand. *Daily Life in a Plains Indian Village 1868*. New York, NY: Clarion, 1999.

Yue, David, and Charlotte Yue. *The Tipi*. New York, NY: Alfred A. Knopf, 1984.

Biographies

Henry, Christopher E. *Ben Nighthorse Campbell—Cheyenne Chief and U.S. Senator*. New York, NY: Chelsea, 1994.

Shaughnessy, Diane, and Jack Carpenter. *Chief Ouray: Ute Peacemaker*. New York, NY: Newbridge, 1997.

Sherrow, Virginia. *Political Leaders and Peacemakers*. New York, NY: Facts on File, 1994.

Traditional Stories/Historical & Contemporary Fiction/ Mysteries/ Plays

Bruchac, Joseph. *Pushing up the Sky: Seven Native American Plays for Children*. New York, NY: Dial, 2000.

Bruchac, Joseph. *The Circle of Thanks: Native American Poems and Songs of Thanksgiving*. Mahwah, NJ: BridgeWater, 1996.

Bunting, Eve. *Cheyenne Again*. New York, NY: Clarion, 1995.

Clark, Ann Nolan. *There Are Still Buffalo* (reprint). Santa Fe, NM: Ancient City, 1992.

Creel, Ann. H. *Water at the blue earth.* Niwot, CO: Roberts Rinehart, 1998.

Crumb, Sally. *Race to the Moonrise: An Ancient Journey.* Ouray, CO: Western Reflections, 1998.

Duke, Kate. *Archaeologists Dig for Clues.* New York, NY: HarperCollins, 1997.

Goble, Paul. *Death of the Iron Horse.* New York, NY: Bradbury, 1987.

Hobbs, Will. *Beardance.* New York, NY: Atheneum, 1993.

Hobbs, Will. *Beardream.* New York, NY: Atheneum, 1997.

Hobbs, Will. *Bearstone.* New York, NY: Atheneum, 1989.

Finley, Mary Peace. *Little Fox's Secret: The Mystery of Bent's Fort.* Palmer Lake, CO: Filter Press, 1999.

Goble, Paul. *Her Seven Brothers* (reprint). New York, NY: Aladdin, 1988.

Goble, Paul. *Remaking the Earth: A Creation Story From the Great Plains of North America.* New York, NY: Orchard, 1996.

Goble, Paul. *Storm Maker's Tipi.* New York, NY: Atheneum, 2001.

Goble, Paul. *The Great Race of the Birds and the Animals.* New York, NY: Bradbury, 1985.

Goble, Paul. *The Gift of the Sacred Dog.* New York, NY: Bradbury, 1980.

Grumman, Jewell, and Gay Matthaei. *The Ledgerbook of Thomas Blue Eagle.* Charlottesville, VA: Thomasson-Grant, 1994.

Isaacs, Sally Senzell. *Life on the Oregon Trail.* Chicago, IL: Heinemann, 2000.

Jeffers, Susan. *Brother Eagle, Sister Sky.* New York, NY: Dial, 1991.

Korman, Susan. *Horse Raid: An Arapaho Camp in the 1800s.* Norwalk, CT: Soundprints and the Smithsonian Institution, 1998.

Lacapa, Kathleen, and Michael Lacapa. *Less than half, more than whole.* Flagstaff, AZ: Northland, 1994.

Loeper, John J. *Meet the Wards on the Oregon Trail.* New York, NY: Benchmark/Marshall Cavendish, 1999.

Mendoza, Patrick M., Ann Strange Owl-Raben, and Nico Strange Owl. *Four Great Rivers to Cross: Cheyenne History Culture, and Traditions.* Englewood, CO: Teacher Ideas Press, 1998.

Ortiz, Simon. *The People Shall Continue (revised).* San Francisco, CA: Children's Book Press, 1998.

Raczek, Linda T. *Rainy's Powwow.* Flagstaff, AZ: Rising Moon/Northland, 1999.

Raczek, Linda T. *The Night the Grandfathers Danced.* Flagstaff, AZ: North-land, 1995.

Rendon, Marcie. R. *Powwow Summer: A Family Celebrates the Circle of Life.* Minneapolis, MN: Lerner, 1996.

Roop, Peter. *The Buffalo Jump.* Flagstaff, AZ: Northland, 1996.

Skurzynski, Gloria, and Alane Ferguson. *Cliff-Hanger.* New York, NY: Scholastic, 1999.

Smith, Cynthia L. *Jingle Dancer.* New York, NY: Morrow, 2002.

Swamp, Chief Jake. *Giving Thanks: A Native American Good Morning Message.* New York, NY: Lee & Low, 1995.

Taylor, Carrie. J. *The Ghost and Lone Warrior: An Arapaho Legend.* Toronto: Tundra, 1991.

Trimble, Stephen. *The Village of Blue Stone.* New York, NY: Macmillan, 1990.

Wyss. Thelma Hatch. *Bear Dancer.* New York, NY: Simon & Schuster, 2005.

Young, Robert. A Personal Tour of Mesa Verde. Minneapolis, MN: Lerner, 1999.

Videos

Anderson, P. (Producer). *Ute legacy.* Ignacio, CO: Southern Ute Tribe/ Colorado Historical Society, 1999.
>*Produced in consultation with the Southern Ute Tribe, this 17 minute video is accurate and very apropriate for the classroom. It provides the story of the Ute people in Colorado from their perspective. It can be purchased for $25.00 from the Southern Ute Museum, 14826 Highway 172, Ignacio, CO 81137 (970-563-9583)*

Denver March Pow*Wow. Castle Rock, CO: Ecliptic Productions, 1999. (53 minutes)
>*Provides a overview of the Denver March Pow*Wow. The explana-tions are not as detailed as they might be for children who know lit-tle about the powwow. It would wise to read a variety of children's books about the powwow before watching the video.*

Mesa Verde National Park (n.d.). [Video]. Whittier, CA: Finley-Holiday Films. (23 minutes)

Mesa Verde National Park: Land of forgotten people and lost cities [Video]. Mesa Verde National Park, CO: Mesa Verde Association, 1987.

These videos were not produced especially for young people, but instead, for a general audience. Teachers should preview them and decide how to use them most effectively.

Websites

Websites change frequently and servers go down. Although all of the following locations provided good information when this book was produced, some may not be accessible now. As a general rule, tribal websites will provide the most accurate information. These sites are generally updated frequently.

Southern Ute Tribe http://www.southern-ute.nsn.us/

Ute Mountain Ute Tribe http://www.utemountainute.com

Northern Arapaho http://www.northernarapaho.com/

Northern Cheyenne http://www.cheyennenation.com

Southern Cheyenne and Southern Arapaho
http://www.cheyenne-arapaho.org

Resources for Adults

Decker, Peter R. *The Utes Must Go!* Golden, CO: Fulcrum, 2004.

Hoig, Stan. *The Sand Creek Massacre.* Norman, OK: University of Oklahoma, 1961.

Jefferson, James, Robert W. Delaney, and Gregory C. Thompson. *The Southern Utes: A Tribal History (2nd Ed.).* Ignacio, CO: Southern Ute Tribe, 1973.

Roberts, Chris. *Powwow Country: People of the Circle.* Missoula, MT: Meadowlark, 1998.

Stands in Timber & Margot Liberty. *Cheyenne Memories.* Lincoln, NE: University of Nebraska, 1967.

Sutter, Virginia. *Tell Me, Grandmother: Traditions, Stories, and Cultures of Arapaho People.* Boulder, CO: University Press of Colorado, 2004.

Waldman, Carl. *Atlas of the North American Indian (Rev.).* New York, NY: Checkmark/Facts on File, 2000.

West, Elliott. *The Contested Plains.* Lawrence, KS. University Press of Kansas, 1998.

Photo and Illustration Sources

All photos of the 2010 Denver March Pow*Wow © 2010 by Don Williams

Photo of grazing bison: http://serc.carleton.edu/images/research_education/native-lands/crow/bison.jpg

Photo of Grand Mesa © 2009 by Don Williams

Map of Four Corners Ancient Puebloans sites: Manitou Cliff Dwellings Museum, P.O. Box 272, Manitou Springs, Colorado 80829 - http://www.cliffdwellingsmuseum.com/sitemap4.htm

Illustration of a Pueblo III kiva (roof removed and in cross section) from *Peoples of the Mesa Verde Region,* by Crow Canyon Archaeological Center, 2011 (illustration by Joyce Heuman Kramer, copyright Crow Canyon Archaeological Center) http://www.crowcanyon.org/EducationProducts/peoples_mesa_verde/pueblo_II_housing.asp

Kiva reconstruction photo released into public domain by the author http://commons.wikimedia.org/wiki/File:Bandelier_Kiva.jpg

Photo of Cliff Palace, Mesa Verde, CO © 2009 by Don Williams

Metate and mano photo: http://upload.wikimedia.org/wikipedia/commons/7/7a/Takalik_Abaj_metate_3.jpg

Ancient Puebloan pottery: http://commons.wikimedia.org/wiki/File:Chaco_Anasazi_canteen_NPS.jpg

petroglyphs photo: http://commons.wikimedia.org/wiki/File:Petroglyphs_in_Valley_of_Fire.JPG

Ute cradleboard photo: Library of Congress http://www.loc.gov/pictures/item/94509883/

Navajo papoose on a cradleboard with a lamb approaching. Window Rock, Arizona. Photographed by H. Armstrong Roberts, ca. 1936. American Indian Select List number 29. From US National Archives http://web.archive.org/web/20050311004623/http://www.archives.gov/research_room/research_topics/native_americans/select_list_029.html

Bandolier Bag: Children's Museum of Indianapolis
http://digitallibrary.imcpl.org/cdm4/document.php?CISO-
ROOT=/tcm&CISOPTR=76&REC=2 used with permission
under a Creative Commons license

Buffalo Hunters: Smithsonian American Art Museum, Gift of Mrs. Joseph
Harrison, Jr. http://en.wikipedia.org/wiki/File:BuffaloHunters.jpg

Buffalo Hunt on the Southwest Plains photograph: Ad Meskens; painting:
John Mix Stanley (1814-1872)
http://en.wikipedia.org/wiki/File:Buffalo_hunt_on_the_South-
western_plains.jpg

Kainai Travois photo: Library and Archives Canada under the reproduction reference number PA-029769 and under the MIKAN ID
number 3192630 Author Rafton-Canning, A.

Sundance Lodge: http://www.clarke.public.lib.ga.us/images/cheyenne.jpg

Storyteller Painting: http://keithdagley.tripod.com/sitebuildercontent/site-
builderpictures/storyteller.jpg

Bent's Fort drawing: http://www.nps.gov/beol/index.htm

Santa Fe Trail map: http://www.socialstudiesforkids.com/
wwww/us/santafetraildef.htm

Oregon Trail Map: http://www.hmdb.org/marker.asp?marker=20724

Chief White Antelope: http://www.powwows.com/gathering/archive

Chief Little Raven:
http://commons.wikimedia.org/wiki/File:Little_Raven_(Hosa,_Y
oung_Crow),_Head_Chief_of_the_Arapaho,_three-quarter-
length,_seated,_1868_-_1874_-_NARA_-_518894.jpg
Author: Soule, William S. (William Stinson), 1836-1908, Photographer (NARA record: 8464480)
Record creator: Department of the Interior. Office of Indian Affairs. (1849 - 09/17/1947)
Date: 1870?
Current location: National Archives and Records Administration,
College Park

Chief Left Hand Bear:
http://en.wikipedia.org/wiki/File:Flickr_-_...trialsanderrors_-
_Left_Hand_Bear,_Oglala_Sioux_chief,_by_Heyn_Photo,_1899.

Sleeping Ute Mountain:
    http://www.integrativestatistics.com/rolphotos5.htm
Buffalo Hunting From Train:
    http://www.loc.gov/pictures/item/2004669992/
Buffalo Skulls: http://en.wikipedia.org/wiki/File:Buffalo_skulls.jpg
Chipeta and Ouray photo: http://upload.wikimedia.org/wikipedia/com-
    mons/2/29/Chief_Ouray_-_Brady-Handy.jpg
Ute Treaty Photo: http://www.greeleyhistory.org/pages/white_river.html
Nathan Meeker Photo:
    http://www.greeleyhistory.org/pages/meeker_story.html
Photo of Native Foods:
    http://www.nativevillage.org/Archives/2012/FEB%202012%20Ne
    ws/682_press5.jpg

List of Activities

Historic Events

Important Historical and Contemporary Figures

Historical Figures

Bent, Charles
p. 98

Bent, George
p. 107

Bent, William
p. 98

Captain Silas S. Soule
photo p. 109; murder of p.109; Sand Creek Massacre p.109

Chief Black Kettle
photo p. 105; Sand Creek Massacre p. 106

Chief Jack House
p. 155

Chief Left Hand Bear
photo p. 106; Sand Creek Massacre p. 106

Chief Little Raven
photo p. 105

Chief Ouray
and Chipeta, photo p. 121; with Ute Chiefs and Chipeta in Washington, photo p. 122; named spokesperson by U.S. Government, p. 121; Treaty of 1868, p. 122

Chief White Antelope
photo p. 104; Sand Creek Massacre p. 107

Chipeta
and Ouray, photo p. 121; with Ute Chiefs and Ouray in Washington, photo p. 122; Chipeta and Change Story p. 127

Colonel John Chivington
p. 106; Sand Creek Massacre pp. 106, 109

Fitzpatrick, Thomas
p. 103

Govenor John Evans
p. 105; Sand Creek Massacre p.109

Meeker, Nathan
photo p. 124; Meeker Incident, p.125

St. Vrain, Ceran
p. 98

Ute Leaders, list
p.120

Contemporary Figures

Chief Ernest House Sr.
p. 158

Dr. Sara Jumping Eagle
p. 161

Grimm, Jay
p. 159

House, Ernest D. Jr.
p. 156

Stories

Made in the USA
San Bernardino, CA
09 December 2013